death,
dying
and the
law

death, dying and the law

EDITED BY
JAMES T. McHUGH

Our Sunday Visitor, Inc./Bishops' Committee for Pro-Life Activities, N.C.C.B.

Nihil Obstat:
Rev. Alphonsus J. Mueller
Censor Librorum

Imprimatur:
✠*Leo A. Pursley, D.D.*
March 22, 1976

ISBN: 0-87973-736-0
Library of Congress Catalog Card Number: 76-10069

Cover Design by James E. McIlrath

Published as a joint project by
Our Sunday Visitor, Inc., and
Bishops' Committee for Pro-Life Activities
National Conference of Catholic Bishops

Printed and bound in the U.S.A. by
Our Sunday Visitor, Inc.
Noll Plaza
Huntington, Indiana 46750

736

Table of Contents

The Authors

Ned H. Cassem, S.J., M.D.

Dr. Cassem is Associate Professor of Psychiatry, Harvard Medical School, and a member of the psychiatry staff at Massachusetts General Hospital. He is also Faculty Consultant, Center for Law and Health Sciences, Boston University, and Director of Residency Training (Psychiatry) at Massachusetts General Hospital.

Rev. James Doyle

Fr. Doyle is Professor of Theology at Kings College in Wilkes Barre, Pennsylvania. He is currently on leave from Kings College to serve as Assistant to the Editor of the Encyclopedia of Bioethics, a project of the Kennedy Institute, Center for Bioethics, Georgetown University, Washington, D.C.

Msgr. James T. McHugh

Msgr. McHugh is the Director of the Bishops' Committee for Pro-Life Activities of the National Conference of Catholic Bishops.

Michael A. Taylor

Michael Taylor is the Associate Director of the Bishops' Committee for Pro-Life Activities of the National Conference of Catholic Bishops.

Foreword

Human life is God's gift to each of us by a loving act of creation. The sanctity of life and the dignity of the individual person is based on the fact that each of us is created in the image of God. From the moment of conception each human life begins its wondrous journey back to the Father. No one has the right to put an end to an innocent life which God meant to grow in the knowledge and love of Himself and meant to share His life and love forever. It is to God that we must answer for what we do or allow to be done to the lives He has created, whether they are already born or are still in the womb. The right to life is at stake at one end of the scale in abortion; at the other end of the scale in euthanasia.

All of our earthly existence — our accomplishments and failures, our sufferings and our joys — are part of the present life which prepares us for eternal union with God. To face the problems of life, and to understand the mystery of death, requires faith and hope. "For," as the Second Vatican Council reminds us, "faith throws a new light on all things and makes known the full ideal which God has set for man, thus guiding the mind towards solutions that are fully human" (*Pastoral Constitution on the Church in the Modern World,* No. 11). The redeeming life, death and resurrection of Jesus Christ offers the promise of an eternity full of the peace and happiness that presently, here on earth, escapes us.

However, we do not always look at human events through the eyes of faith. So often we search instead for natural causes and human reasons to explain the events that shape our lives. We are inclined to measure events more by their impact and relevance here and now, rather than in terms of eternity and immortality.

This is so true when we face the mystery of death. Our instinctive reaction is to recoil from death, to rebel against its seeming finality, to search for some alternative. Human life is so sacred that we gladly expend our energy and our resources to sustain it. We strive to overcome those things that demean life and diminish its dignity — poverty, disease, violence, ignorance. Nonetheless, death does come to each of us, and we must learn to balance the finality of death in human terms with the prospect of eternal life that it opens to us as we consider it from the vantage point of faith and hope.

Although death always remains something of a mystery, the process of dying is a very human experience, and it can often be a moment of true inspiration and actual grace.

This book attempts to assemble scientific and legal information that can be of help in facing the mystery of death and the moral decisions that surround it. For the death of each of us affects — and often involves — all of us. To a very real degree, we share one another's burdens and responsibilities.

Whether we be legislators or jurists, physicians or counselors, nurses or technicians, ministers of faith or members of families, we cannot retreat from invoking moral principles in dealing with the complex and grave problems which confront our society today. Those who, for even the most humanitarian reasons, would relegate to men or to institutions the decision as to who will live and who will die, ignore the fact that God is our Creator and that ultimate decisions over life and death are His prerogative. Indeed they tend to overlook the human ties that bind us to one another and the obligation that we have to care for the sick, the old and the dying.

A true concept of "death with dignity" respects each person as he or she approaches death. It provides that the dying person be subjected to no unnecessary procedures. It allows for alleviation of pain. It gives the dying person the opportunity to prepare spiritually as well as temporally and thus to be at peace.

Decisions about life and death, then, require careful consideration in the context of loving, human relationships. These decisions ought not to be made aside from the community of faith and love in which each person lives. They must be weighed in the light of God's revelation. Guided by the Holy Spirit the Vatican Council said, "It is, therefore, through Christ and in Christ, that light is thrown on the riddle of suffering and death which, apart from His Gospel, overwhelms us. Christ has risen again, destroying death by His death, and has given life abundantly to us so that, becoming sons in the Son, we may cry out in the Spirit: Abba, Father!" (*Pastoral Constitution on the Church in the Modern World,* No. 22).

✝*Terence Cardinal Cooke*

Introduction

We live today in the confusing situation in which advances in medical science have greatly improved our capacity to restore health, or at least to prolong life. At the very same time we are faced with repeated efforts to free us from the responsibility of maintaining life, and to give the appearance of legitimacy to the actual termination of the lives of the aged, the chronically or terminally ill, or those whose existence is no longer considered "meaningful." These counter-trends create ethical dilemmas for the medical profession, and they provoke problems of conscience for the families and friends of those who are dying. A case in point is that of Karen Quinlan.

The Karen Quinlan case in New Jersey involves a young woman who has been in a comatose state since April of 1975 with no apparent hope of regaining consciousness. Miss Quinlan's parents sought an injunction that would allow discontinuing what are generally considered extraordinary means to maintain life, but a New Jersey court has refused the injunction. The court's opinion dealt primarily with procedural issues, and in recent months a number of state legislatures have considered bills that seem to be based on the New Jersey court opinion. Unfortunately, the sudden and determined efforts to write laws are often based on inadequate understanding of the issues involved, poor or deficient research, and not uncommonly, a thirst for publicity.

This book contains a series of essays that attempt to provide a competent medical understanding of the problems of death and dying, to describe the reasons for the legal prohibitions of euthanasia and to clarify the moral and ethical principles. Fr. James Doyle's essay provides the larger context for decisions related to death and dying, and Dr. Cassem clearly describes the realities and the dilemmas that the doctor faces. The essay by the editor presents the Catholic moral teaching on the use of ordinary and extraordinary means to prolong life, and the final chapter by Michael Taylor and the editor provides an analysis of legal approaches and the current status of state laws.

The moral principles on death and dying are part of the heritage of Catholic moral theology, and in recent decades they have been given clearer expression in papal teaching and by the Second Vatican Council. In a 1957 speech to physicians, Pope Pius XII outlined the principle governing the use of ordinary and extraordinary means to preserve life, and the morality of using pain-killing drugs. Although the principle is clear, there is increasing difficulty in applying it in particular cases. The rapid advances in medical science have provided considerably more knowledge about specific diseases, but there remain gaps in our knowledge which might be bridged at any moment, making cure and rehabilitation quite possible. Moreover, the development of medical technology and new "miracle drugs" enables physicians to at least arrest diseases with the likelihood of finding a cure for them in the near future. In effect, the dying patient who today seems beyond the hope of cure and therapy may be restored to health by tomorrow's medical discovery. This realization creates an attitude of caution in many physicians and scientists, and frequently generates hope for the patient's family and loved ones.

In the area of law, most judges, lawyers and legislators are reluctant to have the law bear the full burden of deciding who is to die, or who is to be abandoned by society in his or her dying process. A legal system that provides absolute protection for the right to life of each person and admits no exceptions is consonant with the demands of justice and our constitutional heritage. Yet the law cannot be so sweeping and rigid that it requires prolonging the dying process by any and all means and thereby impedes the dying person from taking leave of his family and meeting his Creator with dignity and grace. The decision not to utilize extraordinary medical procedures to prolong the dying process is ultimately the responsibility and prerogative of the dying person. When the patient is incapable of manifesting that decision, his or her family and loved ones may act in behalf of the patient. But in any case the decision is not simply a medical judgment or a legal prescription. It is a human decision that must be based on respect for human life, and one that is made with moral conviction, compassion and charity.

The purpose of this book is to help people understand how decisions affecting life and death should be made in terms of the Gospel and Christian moral principles, how the dying patient and his or her family might be assisted by the medical and nursing professions, and how respect for life should be protected by the law. It is impossible to supply answers to every problem or dilemma, but the information contained in these pages should help the reader approach the questions of death and dying with confidence tempered by prudence.

Msgr. James T. McHugh

On Death and Dying

by Rev. James Doyle, C.S.C.

Man is only a reed, the feeblest thing in nature; but he is a thinking reed. It is not necessary for the entire universe to take up arms in order to crush him; a vapor, a drop of water is sufficient to kill him. But if the universe crushed him, man would still be nobler than the thing which destroys him, because he knows that he is dying: and the universe which has him at its mercy is unaware of it.

Pascal, *Pensees*

Rediscovering Death

Americans have rediscovered death. At least it would appear so from the steady flow of books and articles on the subject, and from the increase in lectures, workshops and courses on death from coast to coast. Dr. Elizabeth Kübler-Ross, author of *On Death and Dying,* has become almost a household name. Even Marcus Welby, M.D., anguishes about euthanasia before millions of TV viewers.

It was not always so. Not very long ago the subject of death was taboo. Arnold Toynbee has observed that death was considered "un-American" in the United States, that is, it was thought to be a subversive challenge to the American obsession with life, liberty and the pursuit of happiness, as well as a threat to the American cult of health and eternal youth. Only a few years ago Geoffrey Gorer popularized the expression "The Pornography of Death." He made a strong case for the idea that death had replaced sex as the great unmentionable in society. "Never say 'Die' " had come to be taken literally in our culture.

But this has changed greatly in recent years. Several

reasons can be given to explain the current interest in death.

New Medical Technology. It is difficult for many, particularly young people, to fully appreciate the truly revolutionary nature of the new medical technology. Electronic devices (pacemakers and monitoring devices), respirators, antibiotics and many other developments now permit many people to live who would formerly have died. At the start of the century fifteen percent of all newborn infants died in their first year, and nearly another fifteen percent died before adolescence. Today less than two percent die in their first year. Most people live beyond the age of seventy. In industrialized countries today almost two-thirds of those dying die from ailments of old age.

The new technology has been, however, a mixed blessing. Prolonging life has meant in many instances prolonging the dying process. The problem most frequently presents itself as one of medical decision-making at both ends of life, i.e., whether to begin to use or, once begun, to continue to use life-sustaining technology for defective newborns or elderly terminal patients.

Transplantation. The development of transplantation techniques has forced a reconsideration of the legal definition of death. For example, if a still-beating heart is to be taken from a person for transplantation purposes, in what way, if at all, can the donor be called "dead"? If the donor is not dead, would not the surgeon removing the heart be legally guilty of causing the death? What *does* constitute death in the legal sense? This question is the reverse side of the legal question raised in abortion discussions: "When does human life begin?"

The Contemporary "Rights" Movement. American society today is expressing widespread concern for the rights of individuals, and for the protection of these rights against any unwarranted invasion by other individuals or institutions. This trend emphasizes the freedom of the individual and the freedom of personal decision-making. In a medical context, there is consumer concern for the patient's "right to know" — to know his condition and prognosis, and treatments available to him — as well as his right to refuse treatment, even life-sustaining treatment.

It is not uncommon to read and hear today of a "right to die," often asserted without making the necessary distinction between means and end. American law, as interpreted by the courts, is showing less and less inclination to intrude into areas said to be those of private decision and action, thus widening the area of private choice. The "right to privacy," asserted as constitutionally protected in the *Roe v. Wade* and *Doe v. Bolton* abortion decisions, is certain to be invoked as justification for a person's constitutional right to terminate his life. Similarly, it is already being argued by some (and rightly feared by others) that if a person has such a "right to die," others have the obligation to see that the right can be exercised, or at least the obligation not to impede its exercise. The import of this line of reasoning for terminal-care facilities can easily be imagined.

If the unspeakable, death, is now being spoken about more openly and freely, it is equally true that discussion about "what to do with the dying" is more widespread than ever. Increasingly in the last decade, euthanasia (understood here as the direct taking of the life of the seriously ill) has been publicly advocated in circles — medical, philosophical, religious and legal — where it was anathema only a few years ago. "Death with dignity" has become for many a new rallying cry, an apparently harmless and even attractive slogan until one sees the many ambiguities it contains.

The Church's Role

Christians must reflect upon their understanding of death and dying. They should determine in what way they can best witness in word and action to this understanding in American society today. There is a clear parallel here with what is happening with regard to abortion. As the Church cannot restrict itself to denouncing abortion, but must provide realistic alternatives to women contemplating abortion, so it is not enough for the Church to decry the euthanasia movement, but must provide realistic alternatives to those who, fearing a prolonged and subhuman dying process, seriously advocate direct euthanasia as a solution.

The strongest appeal of the euthanasia movement lies in its seeming compassion for the dying. Christians, on the other hand, are often pictured as lacking in compassion. An alternative to euthanasia can be found in the Christian theology of death and in its compassionate pastoral application today.

The Christian and Death: Affirming Life and Affirming Death

"Life" can be considered from many points of view — the biological, the sociological and the theological, to mention only three. "Death" can be considered in similar terms — as the cessation of biological life; as a phenomenon perceived in various ways by various groups and cultures; or as a human experience understood in light of the Christian community's reflection on its faith. From whatever vantage point one begins, however, death remains a profound mystery.

The Christian understanding of death is a "faith-view." This suggests, first, that the Christian view tells the believer something about the mystery of death, but does not completely dispel the mystery. Secondly, the Christian "faith-view," since it is not self-evident, may be quite unintelligible to those who do not share the Christian faith. St. Paul refers to the "foolishness" of the cross. As Fr. Edward Schillebeeckx has written: "On the natural level, the death of a man is indeed an absurd phenomenon, senseless, and unintelligible, something that denies all the promise that man bears within himself in his earthly life and shatters all his inmost hopes." The Christian view is revolutionary: it denies that death is meaningless. . . .

The Gospel sees life existentially; life is a person's saying "yes" or "no" to God, either affirming or negating life and its ultimate meaning. In the Gospel life is either a "going out" of one's self in order to find one's self in the neighbor and in God, or else life is a "turning back upon" one's self, living a life of egoism and selfishness, which results in alienation from others, from God, and even from one's self. Death, then, is a triumph for those who have affirmed life and chosen to say "yes" to God; for "the sinner," i.e., the one who has chosen self over all else, death is the final event of alienation.

Jesus, as true man, took upon Himself "the human condition," including man's mortality. By His death, Jesus conquered and transformed death. He did so by trust and confidence in the Father, and by a steadfast and unwavering conviction that saying "yes" to the Father would give meaning to a seemingly meaningless death. "Father, into thy hands I commend my spirit" (Luke 23:46). What seemed the end was not only not that, but also the beginning of a new life, the risen life of the Lord. As Jesus was delivered from death and restored to His original glory in and through His resurrection, those who "die in the Lord," that is, those who make their own His trust and confidence in the Father, will be "saved," will share in His triumph over death and its seeming meaninglessness and finality. For the Christian, then, death is not only not an end but a beginning, a breakthrough to the fullness of life with the risen Lord.

Christian faith, however, does not imply that the believer is spared all grief and anxiety in the face of approaching death. Death is still "the enemy," even if the Christian is armed with weapons more than capable of defeating the enemy. It is instructive to read Matthew's account of Jesus' own immediate preparation for His death. "Grief and anguish came over him, and he said to them, 'The sorrow in my heart is so great that it almost crushes me. Stay here and watch with me'" (Matthew 26:37-38). The pastoral implications of this are important, as has been noted by Dr. Roy Branson of the Kennedy Institute, Georgetown, in commenting on Dr. Kübler-Ross' suggestions for leading the dying toward "acceptance" of their death. Even faith in the resurrection does not remove the grim reality of death.

One of the many paradoxes of the Christian faith is that, on the one hand, the Christian "affirms life" and does all he can to fight against whatever threatens life — hunger, disease, floods and other natural disasters; while on the other hand, the Christian "affirms death," that is, affirms that he himself is a creature and is therefore mortal, and that it is through the door of death that he must of necessity walk in order to be fully with the Lord. The Christian paradox *par excellence* is that even in "affirming death," one is "affirming life."

Pastoral Application: From Curing to Caring

The Church must witness to its understanding of death in action as well as in word. When the time for curing and recovery has passed, healing in the sense of comforting and supporting the dying must come into play. Dr. Paul Ramsey speaks of "company-ing with" the dying. Wherever people are dying — in tenement flats, in nursing homes, in hospitals — the hope and consolation of the Christian message must be proclaimed.

Norman St. John-Stevas puts it well: "Dying . . . can be a vital period in a person's life, reconciling him to life and death, and giving an interior peace. To achieve this, intense, loving and tactful care and cooperation are needed. . . . This approach to dying is, I believe, more humane and compassionate than the snuffing out proposed by those who may be well-intentioned, but who seem to understand little of the real needs of those they are seeking to help."

Although death can come to a person of any age, suddenly or slowly, the following observations pertain particularly to older patients with more or less prolonged terminal illnesses.

• The dying are best at teaching others how to care for them. Each patient is unique, and reactions to serious illness will differ from patient to patient, as reactions will differ on the part of a given patient during stages of his own illness. While certain generalizations can be made about the dying, it is essential to discover how *this* person is reacting to terminal illness. This can best be done by being alert not only to what the patient is saying, but equally important, to his nonverbal communications and cues as well.

• Two of the leading specialists in the field, Dr. Elizabeth Kübler-Ross, and Dr. Herman Fiefel, have discovered in their practice that, contrary to popular opinion, terminally ill patients generally want to discuss their situation with someone. They resent the conspiracy of silence that so often surrounds them. In general, the patient's receptivity, sensitively discovered, will determine when and how the seriousness of his illness can best be revealed to him, or its existence confirmed since in many cases the patient already knows the truth. Gradual revelation is in all cases to be preferred to a blunt matter-of-fact announcement.

- The counselor must be attuned to the emotions often experienced by the dying patient who knows his diagnosis: denial, anger, fear and anxiety, irritability and hostility, guilt, depression resulting from a sense of isolation from family, friends, work and familiar surroundings. Great patience, understanding, personal maturity and willingness to hear out the patient are required of the counselor, who is frequently made the object of hostility transferred by the patient from some other persons (family or health professionals) or from the institution in which the patient unwillingly finds himself.

- The patient can be reassured against his anxieties. He can be assured that he is not in fact a bother to others, that his life has in fact been worthwhile, that he is not being punished for past wrongdoing, that he can cope with what lies ahead, and that he will not be abandoned by his loved ones. Most patients, according to Dr. Bernard Schoenberg of Columbia University College of Physicians and Surgeons, fear the process of dying more than death itself, i.e., they fear pain that they cannot bear, loss of control of their functions, a kind of regression to infantilism. As one cancer patient put it, "It's not being dead I mind, but the mechanics of dying." Abandonment is felt especially by the untouchables of our society, cancer victims. Doctors and nurses tend to withdraw through a sense of defeat; friends and relatives withdraw through a sense of helplessness. The patient, nevertheless, needs the reassurance that he is still loved.

• Dr. Kübler-Ross has written that "truly religious people with an abiding relationship with God have found it much easier to face death with equanimity" than have others. She is quick to point out, however, that the religious faith of which she is speaking must be authentic and internalized, as opposed to superficial and merely external.

The special assurance of the faith must be made available to the Christian who is dying. Often one's caring presence is enough. At other times a word spoken out of personal faith-conviction carries great comfort. This may be a simple confession of belief in the goodness and kindness of God working mysteriously even in difficult times; it may be a reminder of the redemptive value of the suffering the person is called upon to bear. It might be proper to call to the attention of some patients the "Christian Affirmation of Life" of the Catholic Hospital Associaton. The counselor should not hesitate to suggest prayer, either leading in the recitation of familiar prayers, or equally important, offering personal prayers of faith, hope, love and a desire to accept the divine will. Meditative reading of passages from the Old and New Testaments is usually appropriate. The reception of the sacraments of Penance and the Eucharist can bring great comfort and strength.

The family of the dying person also needs comforting and support. Contemporary society has so emphasized self-control, self-reliance, keeping a "stiff upper lip," that for one to admit sorrow and the need of assistance during the period before and after the death of a loved one is sometimes considered an admission of weakness and immaturity. There is a natural grieving process both before and after a loss. As the Christian "companies-with" the dying, so he "companies-with" the bereaved, witnessing to the fact that grief in no way constitutes a denial of one's faith. Jesus wept when he learned of the death of His friend Lazarus (John 11:35).

Just as no person lives alone, no person dies alone. Death occurs in the world of nature and things, movements and social forces die and pass from memory. But the death of every person, famous or unknown, is an important human and supernatural event, and part of the mystery of life. The Second Vatican Council describes the paradox well:

"It is in the face of death that the riddle of human existence becomes most acute. Not only is man tormented by pain and the advancing deterioration of his own body but even more so by a dread of perpetual extinction. Man rebels against death because he bears in himself an eternal seed which cannot be reduced to sheer matter. . . . Although the mystery of death utterly beggars the imagination, the Church has been taught by Divine Revelation, and herself firmly teaches that man has been created by God for a blissful purpose beyond the reach of earthly misery" (*Pastoral Constitution on the Church in the Modern World*, No. 18).

This essay originally appeared in the 1975 *Respect Life* program manual, published by the Bishops' Committee for Pro-Life Activities of the National Conference of Catholic Bishops.

Death and Dying: Moral and Ethical Considerations

by Msgr. James T. McHugh

In recent years increasing attention has been given to death and dying. It may be a consequence of the growing violence in our society, which has resulted in an early death for many people. It can also be attributed to the scientific progress which has led or promises to lead to the cure of diseases that formerly resulted in death. This same scientific progress has enabled the medical profession to keep people alive, even if only barely so, for a relatively long period of time, even when there is no hope of survival or recovery. Finally, there has also been a growing trend in state legislatures to consider what are euphemistically described as "death with dignity" bills. Other legislative proposals have been concerned with the definition of death in the context of transplantation of organs.

In the face of these events, physicians, moralists and many other concerned persons have begun to reexamine (1) the precise definition of death, and (2) the criteria for determining when efforts to prolong life may legitimately cease.

The physician's interest springs from his concern for the patient and the patient's family. Family and friends are concerned with keeping their trusts of love, companionship or friendship with the patient. The moralist and the private citizen are concerned about the bases on which decisions are made, who takes responsibility for them, and how, in a comfort-oriented society, people will be able to understand the meaning of death and the final events in a dying person's life.

In some cases, attempts to achieve a contemporary understanding of death and dying are but a subterfuge for efforts to permit legal euthanasia or mercy killing. In some places people are being encouraged to sign agreements that will allow physicians to withdraw the support systems that maintain life in a critical situation. Behind much of this is the "quality of life" ethic, according to which the lives of certain persons are considered of inferior quality because of some defect or disadvantage, because of the burden that such persons place on others, or because it is deemed too costly for society to provide care and sustenance to keep them alive.

Scientist Dael Wolfle has briefly stated the questions that physicians and health-care specialists are presently raising:

"Is society ready to analyze death and the prolongation of life in terms of cost-benefit analysis, or to consider shifting the use of expensive facilities from the hopelessly ill to those whose future holds more promise? What about the customary reluctance to administer powerful but addictive drugs until 'near end'? What do we think of the 'senseless prolongation' of life? Birth is no longer blindly accepted, but increasingly is planned and timed. Does this development and the growing acceptance of abortion indicate a readiness to consider euthanasia? The taboo against the discussion of such questions will have to relax, and seems already to be doing so. A society increasingly concerned about the quality of life cannot omit the final chapter from its concern" (*Science*, June 19, 1970).

Some Basic Principles

In developing guidelines for the current public discussion concerning death and the criteria for deciding whether to prolong life, the following principles should serve as the basic presuppositions:

• The life of each person is sacred because God has created each of us, and our spiritual heritage has been merited by the redemptive acts of Jesus Christ. Although human life is personal and unique for each of us, we are not the absolute masters of our existence or of the decisions affecting life or death.

• Death is not merely a physical or social phenomenon, but also an important spiritual event for each person. It is not merely the end of earthly existence, but the beginning of eternal life.

• An important aspect of the care of the dying is spiritual preparation for death. Clergy, family, friends and the medical profession all have a role to play in assisting the dying to see death as a step toward union with God.

• The life of every person is valuable, and society should do all that is necessary to maintain life and restore health to those who are critically ill.

• Christianity has always taught that, although human suffering is not a good in itself, some good may result from it. When associated with the suffering of Christ, no one suffers alone or uselessly. The Second Vatican Council reminds us that the likeness of the suffering Lord is especially apparent in each person who suffers from pain or hardship.

In light of these principles, and of particular problems resulting from the quality of life ethic, there are three specific issues to deal with:

First, a consideration of criteria for determining when death has occurred.

Second, an updating of our understanding of the principles concerning the use of ordinary and extraordinary means to prolong or preserve life.

Third, the application of these principles with regard to children.

When Does Death Occur?

As a result of progress in medical science and medical technology, the possibilities for maintaining life have been expanded considerably. In the vast majority of cases, medical knowledge and life-preserving technology is appropriately used to restore health. However, in some cases, the restoration of health is beyond the realm of possibility, and the use of medical technology then prompts the following ethical questions:

• When a person can no longer be restored to health, and the cessation of life-preserving technology means that death will occur more rapidly, what are the criteria for continuing or discontinuing the use of the technology?

• Since the transplantation of organs often involves obtaining a healthy organ immediately after death has been pronounced, what criteria should be followed to protect patients who are potential organ donors?

Basic to both these questions are the criteria for determining when death occurs. Customarily, physicians considered the absence of respiration and heartbeat as indicative that death had occurred. However, respiration and heartbeat can now be maintained through the use of medical technology, even though the person is beyond any possibility of recovery.

As a consequence, efforts have been made to establish the cessation of brain activity as a new criterion of death. An Ad Hoc Committee of the Harvard Medical School to Examine the Definition of Brain Death, under the chairmanship of Henry K. Beecher, M.D., in 1968 issued a report on *A Definition of Irreversible Coma*. This report listed four characteristics of irreversible coma, that, if verified, would constitute brain death. Those characteristics are:

• *Unreceptivity and unresponsitivity.* The patient shows no awareness of and no response to externally applied stimuli, even of the most sensitive or painful nature.

• *No movements or breathing.* The patient, under continuous observation by physicians for at least one hour, shows no spontaneous muscular movements, no spontaneous respiration, and no response to external stimuli. When a respirator is used, the absence of spontaneous respiration for three minutes when the respirator is turned off, confirms the lack of respiratory ability.

• *No reflexes.* The absence of specific elicitable reflexes is further evidence of the absence of central nervous system activity.

• *Flat electroencephalogram.* This test is of great value in confirming the absence of brain activity and thus of brain death.

According to the Harvard group, the examination should be repeated twenty-four hours later after the initial diagnosis to verify that all four conditions are met and are unchanged. Furthermore, the Harvard criteria are not to be relied upon when the patient has taken depressant drugs.

A Task Force on Death and Dying of the Hastings Institute of Society, Ethics and the Life Sciences reviewed the Harvard criteria in 1972, and substantially supported them. The Institute group emphasized that all four characteristics should be present, and they warned against sole or undue reliance on the flat electroencephalogram. Paul Ramsey, in *The Patient as Person* (1970), also cautions that the Harvard criteria, in the presence of natural circulation and respiratory function, are not conclusive.

In summary, then, the following approaches to determining death are customarily accepted by the medical profession:

• Cessation of natural circulation and respiratory activity. Circulation and respiration are considered the "basic vital signs" by physicians, and in the vast majority of cases their absence is sufficient to determine that death has occurred.

• In cases of irreversible coma, the Harvard Committee criteria are generally accepted as indicating that the patient is dead.

• A flat electroencephalogram, of and by itself, is insufficient to determine that a patient is dead.

Easily accessible and absolutely infallible criteria of death are still not available, and the development of new and increasingly sophisticated technology for sustaining life makes their realization ever more difficult and tenuous. The medical profession has always had to live with the absence of certitude, and threats of malpractice and attempts to legally define death create new tensions. Given the present uncertainties in medicine and ethics, lawmakers and judges should exhibit a proper humility and caution.

Ordinary and Extraordinary Means to Preserve Life

Distinguishing between "ordinary" and "extraordinary" means has become commonplace in discussing the obligation to prolong life when a person is irremediably ill and death is certain.

Citing Pope Pius XII for his assertion of the principle, moralists and ethicians hold that we must take all ordinary means to preserve life, even if there is little hope of recovery. We are not obliged to use extraordinary means to prolong life when recovery is no longer possible, although we may do so.

Ordinary means are described as "all medicines, treatments and operations which offer a reasonable hope of benefit for the patient and can be obtained and used without excessive pain, expense, or other inconveniences."

By extraordinary means are meant "all medicines, treatments and operations which cannot be obtained or used without excessive expense, pain or other inconvenience, or which if used would not offer a reasonable hope of benefit."

Thus by extraordinary means we mean all medicines, treatments and operations:

- which will not cure the pathology, but will restrain its progressive destruction;
- which offer no sure hope of cure, and may involve a significant risk;
- which, if successful, render the patient incapable of certain functions;
- which are extremely painful;
- which are extremely expensive.

It is important to keep in mind that the criteria for "extraordinary means" are flexible and changing. We must avoid too rigid a categorization of such means. Generally, pain is only temporary, and drugs can be used to minimize its effect. Also, expense is a highly relative factor, and one that receives disproportionate importance in a materialistic society. Health-care insurance can make medical care available to all, regardless of wealth.

Therefore, this is very much a working principle whose terms are subject to continued redefinition. It must be constantly reexamined, especially in light of scientific discoveries, increased expertise in surgical procedures and developments in medical technology. Means of preserving life that are looked upon as extraordinary at a given time or in given circumstances may become quite ordinary and commonplace in a short period of time.

The Quality of Life and Children

In its tragic opinions of January 22, 1973, striking down state abortion laws, the Supreme Court cited "health reasons" that would justify ending the life of the fetus, not only during the first six months of pregnancy but also during the last three months when the child can usually survive with ordinary incubational care. The court listed the following reasons related to the mother's health as sufficient to permit destroying the fetus:

• "Maternity, or additional offspring, may force upon the woman a distressful life and future."

• "Psychological harm may be *imminent.*"

• "Mental and physical health may be taxed by child care."

• "There is also the distress, *for all concerned,* associated with the unwanted child."

• "The additional difficulties and continuing stigma of unwed motherhood may be involved."

Each of these reasons can be applied to the newborn infant, as well as to the unborn child. In fact, it takes little imagination to reconstruct the list so that it could also be applied to an incurably ill person as well. Thus:

• The suffering of the incurably ill may force upon the family a distressful life and future.

• Psychological harm (for spouse, children, relatives) may be imminent.

• Mental and physical health may be taxed by caring for the sick person.

• There is also the distress, for all concerned, associated with the dying process of the patient.

• The additional difficulties and continuing stigma (of alcoholism, drug-use, loss of bodily functions) may be involved.

Moreover, the court in *Wade* and *Bolton* recognized only "the potentiality of human life" for the fetus during the last three months of pregnancy. The court was able to permit the destruction of the fetus at any point because it had already decided that "the unborn have never been recognized as persons in the whole sense," and that decisions as to the value of human life in the womb were based on presumptions concerning "the capability of meaningful life outside the womb." It is this last point, "capability of meaningful life," that can be used as a weapon against the aged, sick or incurably ill.

In the past two years a number of cases involving decisions to allow — or cause — infants or very young children to die have come to public attention. In Baltimore, a mongoloid child with multiple defects needed a relatively simple operation to survive. The operation was refused by the parents.

In Yale New Haven Hospital, forty-three physically or mentally impaired infants in need of some corrective surgery or special care were allowed to die. At least in some cases the doctors felt that if the child had lived, it would have had little hope of achieving meaningful life.

In Boston, a child who survived an abortion reportedly died as a result of a positive act or of determined neglect, because the doctor did not consider the child "viable."

In some of these cases it may have been permissible to withhold the extraordinary means to sustain life, because the child would not have been cured by its use, and because the most that could be accomplished would be a short prolongation of life.

However, in each of these cases a strongly influencing

factor — if not the principal motivating factor — was that the child also suffered from other disabilities, mental or physical. Thus, the decision to withhold therapy was at least partially the expression of the judgment that this life was not of sufficient value to save. And in the calculus, it was also apparent that the burdens resulting from continued life would have fallen more heavily on the parents and society than on the child. Almost imperceptibly we have passed from the rights of the patient to the problems of society, and to a situation in which cost-benefit analysis results in destroying the life of the child.

In summary, the following conclusions emerge:

• The Church should see a special pastoral responsibility and mission in preparing people for death. This includes compassion and empathy, the availability of the sacraments, and fostering understanding of human suffering as associated with the suffering Christ.

• Catholic hospitals, physicians, nurses and health-care workers should be in the forefront of pastoral care of the terminally ill and the dying.

• In determining when to cease using extraordinary means to prolong life, the patient has the primary right to decide. Physicians, clergy, family and friends should assist the patient in making the decision and should help the patient in the dying process.

• Because of the dangers involved, and because of the multiple roles the physician plays (curing the patient, caring for the patient, overcoming disease, increasing the storehouse of scientific information), the physician alone should not make the decision about prolonging life. Moreover, to protect the patient's rights, physicians should take a conservative approach in applying the principles to individual cases.

Conclusion

At best, there will be a tragic element in every death. Suffering, sorrow, human regret and the sense of loss will not be done away with completely. Physicians and health-care workers should do all that is reasonably possible to ease suffering. The Church, through its ministers, should balance sorrow with Christian hope. Family and friends should help those closest to the dying person to cope with and overcome the effects of death.

This essay originally appeared in the 1974 *Respect Life* program manual, published by the Bishops' Committee for Pro-Life Activities of the National Conference of Catholic Bishops. The essay has been revised and updated for inclusion in *Death, Dying and the Law.*

Controversies Surrounding the Hopelessly Ill Patient

by Ned H. Cassem, S.J., M.D.

When does our medical treatment of dying patients become unjustified abuse? During the last seventy hours of his life in Siskiyou General Hospital, California, Emil A. Liloiva accumulated a medical bill in excess of $10,000. His treatment included two unsuccessful cardiac operations. After his death, the County Administrator rejected the hospital's claim for the portion of the patient's bill related to those final three days.[1] This is perhaps the first of several lawsuits against hospitals arguing that certain treatment of irreversibly ill patients was unjustified. Elliot Slater[2] pointed out that the two goals of medicine — the relief of suffering and the preservation of health — can become, for the dying patient, mutually contradictory. The proportion of irreversibly ill persons in whom this dilemma may exist is suggested by data from England indicating that not less than sixty-eight percent of the deaths in that country occurred after a long illness, predominantly stroke and cancer.[3] Not less than half of those individuals were over seventy-five years of age.

Reflecting the recent surge of national protest against hospitals and physicians for unnecessarily prolonging life in this category of patient, Abelson[4] wrote, "Death of a loved one was bad enough when it was in the hands of

God; now it is often a much more distressing experience."
When using heroic measures to treat terminally ill patients,
physicians are increasingly accused of inhumanity, experi-
mentation, cruelty and/or biological idolatry. *U.S. News
and World Report* (May 22, 1972), *Time* (July 16, 1973),
Atlantic (February 1974), *New York Times Magazine* (June
23, 1974), and many other popular articles, along with Pat-
rick Henry and euthanasia societies from coast to coast,
proclaim that "death with dignity" is often preferable to
life without it. Celebrities have endowed this movement for
"death with dignity" with credibility and considerable im-
petus. Medical Nobel Laureate Sir Macfarlane Burnet, for
example, stated: "Death in the old should be accepted as
something always inevitable and sometimes positively desirable. Doctors should not compel old people to die more
than once." To emphasize his endorsement he carried a
card with the message: "I request that, in view of my age
(73), any prolonged unconsciousness, whether due to ac-
cident, heart attack or strokes, should be allowed to take
its course without benefit of an intensive-care or resuscitation ward."

Indeed some blame the advancement of modern technological devices for treatment now available in hospitals
for creating an "ethical crisis." On Saturday evening, January 5, 1974, ABC television network further publicized
the dilemma of persons with terminal illness by showing
"ABC News Close-up: The Right To Die." This program
highlighted the fact that some persons have felt it so necessary to protect themselves from excessive treatment when
they are hopelessly ill that they are signing Living Wills.
Since 1969 the Euthanasia Education Council has distrib-
uted more than a quarter million of these documents. Legislation to make them legally binding has been introduced
in Delaware, Oregon, Montana, Massachusetts, Idaho, Il-

linois, West Virginia and Florida. Currently the U.S. House of Representatives is considering bill HR 2655, which would establish a Commission on Medical Technology and Dignity of Dying.

In response to similar pressures the New York Academy of Medicine on December 20, 1972, issued an official statement, "Measures Employed to Prolong Life in Terminal Illness." The statement pointed out that traditional religious ethics have always recognized there is no obligation on the part of a physician to use heroic measures to prolong life in hopelessly ill patients, and that there is no prohibition against the use of narcotics to ease pain even though such medication may shorten life. The statement urged that consideration be given to the following:

• Mere preservation of life must not be the sole objective of treatment.

• The physician should discuss the situation with the patient or family and should encourage both the patient and the family to express their feelings and wishes.

• The opinions and recommendation of the family physician should be obtained even if he is not a physician of record in the particular case.

• The views of religious advisers may be helpful.

To conclude: When, in the opinion of the attending physician, measures to prolong life which have no realistic hope of effecting significant improvement will cause further pain and suffering to the patient and the family, we support conservative, passive medical care in place of heroic measures in the management of a patient afflicted with a terminal illness.[5]

Catholic Moral Tradition

"Euthanasia" is such an inflammatory word that its use occasionally makes rational discussion impossible.

However, most of the proponents of "death with dignity" favor *negative* (or passive) euthanasia — allowing a person to die naturally from an already fatal illness. As early as 1957, Pope Pius XII stated that there was no moral obligation to use extraordinary means to prolong life in hopelessly ill patients, and added that agents such as narcotic analgesics could be administered to relieve suffering, even though their use might shorten the life of the patient.[6] Traditional moral and medical teaching has almost universally regarded *positive* (or active) euthanasia — direct administration of a lethal agent, such as potassium chloride — as unethical and forbidden. The distinction which differentiates potassium chloride from morphine given to relieve pain includes both the intention of the physician (to relieve pain rather than to kill) and the effects of the drug. Potassium chloride, when administered in lethal dose, has no beneficial effects. Williams, in a survey of physicians six years ago, found that eighty-nine percent stated they were in favor of negative euthanasia and eighty percent admitted to having practiced it. Only fifteen percent favored positive euthanasia.[7] Few physicians regard the mere existence of elaborate technological devices as a moral mandate for their use on all mortally ill patients.

In fact, St. Christopher's Hospice in London has gained international fame for offering a facility in which terminal patients can die comfortably without, in some cases, so much as an intravenous line if the latter is not warranted.[8] Why then does the public behave as though the opportunity to die comfortably will be denied them by physicians and hospitals?

Fears of Terminal Abuse and Loss of Dignity

Medical science has in no way slowed its technological advance. Bypass grafts, intraaortic balloon pumps, membrane oxygenators, advances in transplantation and other forms of surgery, new drugs against microbial and malignant invaders, plus increasingly sensitive monitoring devices for all who survive the heroic treatments — all now offer chances of survival that approach the miraculous. Persons who would have surely died — and before might never have been treated — are now given whatever chance they have in the operating room or ICU. The condition is worse to start with, and failure is common. Because the new technologies are commonly painful and usually awkward, families of the dead often question in retrospect whether the last-ditch effort was worth it. Were the final heroics only a humiliation inflicted on an individual whose demise was inevitable anyway? Couldn't he have died more comfortably, even with dignity, without them?

The calculus is therefore simple: persons in increasingly desperate straits are being given better chances of survival, and the crowd who lingers with this hope at the brink of death has swollen. It is a time of tremendous stress both for the sick and those who take care of them. Frustrations become accusations: doctors preserve life merely for its own sake, experiment for their gains, or commit murders of convenience; good money is being squandered on hopeless cases; healthy younger persons are excluded from ICU beds occupied by the unsalvageable; society's resources are being wasted, etc. But society continues to demand care and the chance to live, forgetting that indignity may well be an inevitable part of the gamble. More persons are taking the gamble, and, like soldiers, increasing numbers survive the conflict but have lost the war. They and their families ask, "Death is bad enough, why make it worse?"

Most persons have no desire to have their body's life maintained long after irreversible brain damage has occurred. Of course, if a person could be proved dead, then most would agree artificial support of organs is not justified. With increasing demand for transplant patient donors, pressure to define when a person is dead became intense. Because the ethical code requires that the donor be dead before organs are to be removed before transplantation, a major contribution came with the Harvard criteria of brain death: absence of receptivity or responsivity, no spontaneous movements or breathing, no reflexes, and an isoelectric EEG, all repeated at two intervals twenty-four hours apart.[9] (This definition of death is not recognized by civil law in any state except Kansas,[10] Maryland, and in a special way Connecticut.[11]) Despite criticism of the inclusion of EEG data among the criteria[12-14] defining death, the essence of the concept remains intact leaving the conscientious physician with a set of criteria for judging clinical death. But a paradox remains.

In Palm Springs General Hospital, Hialeah, Florida, Mrs. Carmen Martínez, seventy-two, suffering from longstanding hemolytic anemia, asked her physician, Dr. Rolando López, to spare her a splenectomy and all further cutdowns. When Dr. López sought a court decision about granting her wish, Judge David Popper of Miami ruled that she had a right to refuse the treatment.[15] Skillman[16] argues that physicians are forced to make decisions about continuing or stopping heroic measures long before brain death occurs. Like Mrs. Martínez, increasing numbers request not to be kept alive until their brains are dead.

Why the Opposition to 'Death with Dignity'?

Despite widespread general opposition to prolongation of life at any cost in an illness already irreversible, the "death with dignity" movement, as well as Living Wills, has met considerable resistance. Several important factors appear to be involved.

1. *The Moral Domino Theory.* Increasing attention has been given of late to the "slippery slopes" of science.[17] According to this position, the power to decide for death over life will corrupt its possessors, lead to direct (active or "mercy") killing of patients, and progress to genocide or other forms of mass extermination. The first fear received some support on the level of ethical theory for while most moral philosophers and theologians like Ramsey[18] and McCormick[19] sharply distinguish the positive (active) from negative (passive) euthanasia, Joseph Fletcher[20-21] regards the two as identical. Most recently Rachels[22] argues the distinction has no moral importance in that active euthanasia is more humane in many cases than passive euthanasia. Charles Curran[23] also regards the two as identical, but only after the dying process (which he does not define) has begun. Therefore, it might seem that we would be empowering some persons to do away with others (see point 4 below). Furthermore, those opposed to "opening the door" to legalization of Living Wills or passive euthanasia perhaps fear that it will open a slippery slope destined to end in practices little different from those of Nazi Germany — a consummation devoutly to be shunned.[24]

2. *Difficulty Defining Irreversibility.* When is an illness irreversible? Even if we knew the probabilities of survival which are appropriate — five percent? one percent? — a different set of criteria would have to be developed for every illness or at least for each type of organ failure (e.g., heart, liver, kidneys). Imperfect knowledge in these areas causes many physicians to hesitate before discontinuing treatment efforts.

3. *Accomplice to Suicide.* Some have feared that legalization of Living Wills may leave those who comply with

their requests open to the charge of their being accomplices to a suicide.

4. *Limitation of Care.* Dyck[25] has argued that the vagueness of the label "hopeless" tends to justify the limitation of care because hopeless connotes meaningless. Because the lives of irreversibly ill persons might be construed as meaningless, the care given them would be limited. For example, the old could be morally coerced to forgo heroic surgery.

5. *Distrust of Human Nature.* Successful execution of Living Wills presupposes that those responsible for the life of the signer act in his best interest. That is, the signer would not be allowed to die just because he was cantankerous, because he arrived in the emergency ward at 2 a.m., because the hospital census was too full, etc. There are those who believe that this is too much to ask of human nature, for the same reason that it is too much to expect that every nursing home resemble St. Christopher's Hospice.

Reaction of the American Medical Association

Perhaps the above and other reasons prompted the cautious response of medical societies in general and the American Medical Association (AMA) in particular to the question of "death with dignity." The interest of the AMA became clear when its Judicial Council sponsored the Fourth National Congress on Medical Ethics, April 26-28, 1973, although its scope was considerably broader than the "right to die." Specific treatment of the questions of active and passive euthanasia came when, at its December 1973 convention in Anaheim, California, the AMA condemned "mercy killing." Although opposing efforts to obtain a legal definition of the moment of death, they adopted the following resolution on "death with dignity":

"The cessation of the employment of extraordinary means of prolonging the life of the body when there is irrefutable evidence that biological death is imminent is the decision of the patient and/or his immediate family."

Furthermore, although there has been great reluctance, for medico-legal reasons, to record orders like "DNR" (Do Not Resuscitate) or "CMO" (Comfort Measures Only) in the chart or order book, the American Medical Association has very recently recommended such a practice. In a recent supplement to their *Journal* entitled "Standards for Cardiopulmonary Resuscitation (CPR) and Emergency Cardiac Care (ECC)," the following statement was made:

"The purpose of cardiopulmonary resuscitation is the prevention of sudden unexpected death. Cardiopulmonary resuscitation is not indicated in certain situations, such as in cases of terminal irreversible illness where death is not unexpected or where prolonged cardiac arrest dictates the futility of resuscitation efforts. Resuscitation in these circumstances may represent a positive violation of an individual's right to die with dignity. When CPR is considered to be contraindicated for hospital patients, it is appropriate to indicate this in the patient's progress notes. It also is appropriate to indicate this on the physician's order sheet for the benefit of nurses and other personnel who may be called upon to initiate or participate in cardiopulmonary resuscitation."

How Does One Decide to Forgo Heroic Measures?

Even though there may be unanimous agreement that there's a time to stop trying to prolong life and evidence that eighty percent of physicians have at some time done so,[26] there are no unanimous guidelines for discharging this awesome responsibility. Two oversimplified and premature, if convenient, methods are the economic solution and the effort to define quality of life by defining who qualifies for personhood.

The economic solution is now employed in certain provinces of Canada, where each hospital is given a budget and told simply to decide how they wish the money to be spent. The utilization of facilities for the hopelessly ill must then be weighted against their use for "more salvageable" persons. Of course the hope is that the hospital will then be forced to find the most responsible and humane solution to their life-and-death dilemmas. However, each decision to stop the fight against a lethal illness has moral technological (or medical), legal and psychosocial considerations as well as economic ones. To assert that the economic factors should be the sole or primary determinants of policy is surely a distortion of priorities as well as an oversimplification of a complex and grave issue. Furthermore, selection of a sole economic criterion by a wealthy nation like the United States which spends billions on methods of destroying health and lives, is open to serious question.

The "quality of life" solution seeks to help by defining the marks of human personhood so that "mere biological life" need not be prolonged. Joseph Fletcher is probably the best known proponent of this effort and includes among defining marks of "humanhood": minimal intelligence (I.Q. greater than 40); ability to communicate with others; control of existence; self-awareness; self-control; curiosity; a sense of past, present and future; creativity/changeability; distinctiveness; a balance of rationality and feeling; and neocortical functioning.[27] In addition to the specters awaiting us at the foot of the "slippery slope" descending from this formulation, it shares all the follies of pure abstractions. Even though infants, our patients, our spouses, our colleagues or ourselves might not qualify as persons under these criteria, the decision to let an individual die is not necessarily clarified by their application. We would do well to heed Ingelfinger's warning: "As there are few atheists in foxholes, there tend to be few absolutists at the bedside."[28]

Must we then say nothing ethically? McCormick[29] reminds us that failure to seek guidelines for these decisions leaves only the alternatives either of dogmatism or of pure concretism. There must be some line that can be drawn between vitalism (life at any cost) and pessimism (death when life becomes frustrating, burdensome, useless). Both extremes are based on an idolatry of life. McCormick used life as a relative good and the duty to preserve it a limited one. McCormick formulates life as a value to be preserved only where it contains some essential for human relationships. When, because of the condition of the individual, this potential would be completely subordinated to the mere effort for survival, then the life can be said to have achieved its potential.

Are there any practical guidelines to help determine when the time has come to halt efforts to prolong life? Collins[30] has employed a Dying Score derived from evaluation of five physiological parameters (cerebral function, reflexes, respiration, circulation, cardiac action) to study irreversibility of illness in patients following resuscitation.

Two extremely important contributions toward the further study and understanding of the components of life-and-death decisions in critical care settings were recently presented in *Critical Care Medicine*. Cullen et al[31] presented a method for quantifying the energy expenditure in caring for ICU patients, both in terms of procedures performed and in number of personnel devoted to the effort. The Therapeutic Intervention Scoring System (TISS) provides a powerful tool for quantifying the intensity of effort invested in a critically ill person. The authors do not suggest even that it be used in deciding which patients should or should not be vigorously treated. What they provide is an invaluable measure for relating intervention, cost, and use of personnel to efforts at reversing specific potentially lethal conditions. The TISS may help us answer the crucial question of what we can or cannot accomplish by medical technology in the effort to restore health.

Tagge et al[32] presented what appears to be the most promising method yet for deciding responsibly when specific interventions are no longer reasonable. This Mount Sinai classification of patient-care categories avoids entirely the pitfalls of *a priori* criteria which must be met in order for a decision to be made to decrease the intensity of care given to a critically ill person. Its genius lies in its establishment of a process, openly acknowledged and regularly exercised, by which the entire treatment (ICU) team is forced to confront the question of what is best for the whole person in question. As such, the real question initially introduced — is our intervention, in fact, abuse disguised as treatment? — is forced from the shadows of taboo and secrecy and confronted in a way that guarantees (even forces) open, maximal communication. It seems clear from the experience at our own hospital that almost all the disputes over whether a terminally ill patient should be treated more or less intensively have arisen because communication was faulty. One, of course, could argue that the team as a whole could be corrupted by possession of such arbitrary power. However, when the family and the patient (whenever conscious) are partners to the decision, the threat of the "slippery slope" is far less likely.

Talk of a dignified death may be, in fact, a form of self-delusion. Suffering, painful separation, grief and anguish are seldom entirely absent from any death regardless of our efforts to wish it away by slogans.[33-34] There may be an illusion in the minds of some that once the decision is made and no further heroics will be used, all difficulties are solved. That point is precisely where they are most likely to begin and where most care and attention need be given to both patient and family. The responsibility for making decisions to continue or omit extreme measures is awesome enough. After they have been made, the delicate and sensitive issues of human suffering and loss demand even more compassion and courage to continue care under those circumstances. Young physicians and nurses need more guidance in discharging these responsibilities. What our colleagues have confronted alone in past centuries we must now face together.

References

1. *American Medical News,* December 16, 1974, p. 2.

2. Slater, E., "New Horizons in Medical Ethics: Wanted — A New Approach," *British Medical Journal* 1:285-286, 1973.

3. *Reports on Health and Social Subjects* No. 5 (1973). "Care of the Dying, H.M.S.O.," cited by K. O. A. Vickery. "Euthanasia," *Royal Society of Health Journal* 94:118-126, 1974.

4. Abelson, P., "Anxiety About Genetic Engineering," *Science* 173-285, 1971.

5. Abelson, P., *Bulletin New York Academy of Medicine* 49:349-351, 1971.

6. Pius XII, "Pope Speaks — Prolongation of Life," *L'Osservatore Romano* 4:393-398, 1957. [See also Appendix "E" of this book.]

7. Williams, R. H., "Our Role in the Generation, Modification, and Termination of Life," *Archives of Internal Medicine* 124:215-237, 1969.

8. Saunders, C., "A Therapeutic Community: St. Christopher's Hospice," in *Psychological Aspects of Terminal Care,* ed. by B. Schoenberg, A. C. Carr, et al (New York: Columbia University Press, 1972), pp. 275-289.

9. Beecher, H. K., et al, "A Definition of Irreversible Coma," *JAMA* 205:337-340, 1968.

10. Kennedy, I. McC., "The Kansas Statute on Death — An Appraisal," *New England Journal of Medicine* 285:946-949, 1971.

11. Fabro, J. A., letter in *New England Journal of Medicine* 286:549-550, 1972.

12. Beecher, H. K., "Ethical Problems Created By the Hopelessly Ill Patient," *New England Journal of Medicine* 278: 1425-1430, 1968.

13. Moore, F. D., "Medical Responsibility for the Prolongation of Life," *JAMA* 206:384-386, 1968.

14. Mohandas, A., and Chon, S. N., "Brain Death: Clinical and Pathological Study," *Journal of Neurosurgery* 35:211-218, 1971.

15. Reported in *Chicago Sun Times,* July 4, 1971.

16. Skillman, J. J., "Ethical Dilemmas in the Care of the Critically Ill," *Lancet* 2:634-637 (Sept. 14, 1974).

17. Etzioni, A., "The 'Slippery Slope' of Science," *Science* 183 (March 15, 1974).

18. Ramsey, P., *The Patient as Person* (New Haven: Yale University Press, 1970), pp. 157-164.

19. McCormick, R. A., "The New Medicine and Morality," *Theology Digest* 21:308-321, 1973.

20. Fletcher, J., *Moral Responsibility: Situation Ethics at Work* (Philadelphia: Westminster Press, 1967).

21. Fletcher, J., "Ethics and Euthanasia," *American Journal of Nursing* 73:670-675, 1973.

22. Rachels, J., "Active and Passive Euthanasia," *New England Journal of Medicine* 292:78-80, 1975.

23. Curran, C. E. *Politics, Medicine and Christian Ethics* (Philadelphia: Fortress, 1973), pp. 152-163.

24. Alexander, L., "Medical Science Under Dictatorship," *New England Journal of Medicine* 241:39-47, 1949.

25. Dyck, A. J., "An Alternative to the Ethic of Euthanasia," in R. H. Williams' (ed.) *To Live and To Die: When, Why, and How* (New York: Springer-Verlag, 1974), pp. 98-112.

26. Alexander, L., *JAMA* 227:864, 1974.

27. Fletcher, J., "Indicators of Humanhood: A Tentative Profile of Man," *Hastings Center Report* 2:1-4, 1972.

28. Ingelfinger, F. J., "Bedside Ethics for the Hopeless Case," editorial in *New England Journal of Medicine* 289:914-915, 1973.

29. McCormick, R. A., "To Save Or Let Die: The Dilemma of Modern Medicine," *JAMA* 229:172-176, 1974.

30. Collins, V. J., "Considerations in Defining Death," *Linacre Quarterly* 38:94-101, 1971.

31. Cullen, D. J., Civetta, J. M., Briggs, B. A., and Ferrara, L. C., "Therapeutic Intervention Scoring System: A Method for Quantitative Comparison of Patient Care," *Critical Care Medicine* 2:57-60, 1974.

32. Tagge, G. F., Adler, D., Bryan-Brown, C. W., and Shoemaker, W. C., "Relationship of Therapy to Prognosis in Critically Ill Patients," *Critical Care Medicine* 2:61-63, 1974.

33. Ramsey, P., "The Indignity of 'Death With Dignity,' " *Hastings Center Studies* 2:47-62, 1974.

34. Ingelfinger, F. J., "Empty Slogans for the Dying," editorial in *New England Journal of Medicine* 291:845-846, 1974.

This chapter of the book originally appeared in the May 1975 issue of *Linacre Quarterly,* the journal of the National Federation of Catholic Physicians' Guilds, and is reprinted here with permission.

Death and Dying: Analysis of Legislative Approaches

by Msgr. James T. McHugh
and
Michael A. Taylor

In recent years, a number of states have begun to consider laws dealing with death and dying. Among the reasons given for the proposed laws are the growing practice of organ transplantation, the need to protect doctors from malpractice suits, and the necessity to legally specify when the use of extraordinary medical technology is no longer required to prolong life in the face of imminent death.

At present, there is a surge of activity in state legislatures to establish laws. This activity can be expected to increase because of the visibility given to recent court cases, notably the Karen Quinlan case in New Jersey. The bills in the various state legislatures fall into one of three general categories — transplantation of organs, definition of death, death with dignity — and the response to each is different.

Transplantation of Organs

Though directed primarily toward regulating the circumstances of organ transplants — including informed consent of the donor — these bills often include some reference to the verification of death for the donor. These laws generally follow the Uniform Anatomical Gift Act of the National Conference of Commissioners of Uniform State Laws, adopted by the conference and approved by the American Bar Association in 1968. By 1974, virtually all states had adopted the Uniform Anatomical Gift Act (see Appendix "A").

Definition of Death

These bills establish criteria for death (a) to protect physicians who wish to perform transplant operations; (b) to indicate when resuscitative therapy should be initiated or may be discontinued; and (c) to indicate when life-prolonging procedures for an unconscious, dying patient may be withdrawn.

On February 24, 1975, the American Bar Association (ABA), responding to activity to establish statutes in the various states throughout the country, adopted a resolution entitled *A Current Definition of Death.* That resolution states: "For all legal purposes, a human body with irreversible cessation of total brain function, according to usual and customary standards of medical practice, shall be considered dead." The committee that prepared the resolution maintained that the resolution encompasses all existing criteria of death, that is, brain, heartbeat and respiration. Respecting the role of the physician to determine or verify that death has occurred, those supporting the ABA resolution also emphasized the need of a legal definition for the guidance of lawyers, judges and legislators.

In 1973, the American Medical Association (AMA) adopted a recommendation "stating that statutory definition of death is neither desirable nor necessary and suggesting that state medical societies urge their legislatures to postpone enactment of statutes defining death. At that time, the House (of Delegates) reaffirmed a prior policy statement that 'death shall be determined by the clinical judgment of the physician using the necessary available and currently accepted criteria' " (*American Medical News,* October 6, 1975).

In 1974, the AMA House of Delegates adopted a resolution stating that "permanent and irreversible cessation of the brain constitutes one of the various criteria which can be used in the medical diagnosis of death." (Note that this statement does not replace earlier policies, and it emphasizes that cessation of brain function is only "one of the various criteria" for determining that death has occurred.) The medical profession is reluctant to back away from cessation of circulation and respiration as the customary signs of death because in the vast majority of cases these criteria are satisfactory. Moreover, verifying the cessation of brain activity is more difficult and often not possible, and many physicians feel that if it becomes mandatory, it will place undue pressure on physicians and the families of dying or dead patients.

By the end of 1975 at least seven states had enacted new statutes defining death: Kansas (1970), Maryland (1972), Virginia (1973), California (1974), and in 1975, Illinois, Michigan and Oregon (see Appendix "A"). An exclusively legal approach tends to be minimalist and is fraught with danger. Nonetheless, we should anticipate increased interest in establishing state laws that define death, and caution and prudence are qualities that should shape the politico-legal process.

Thus, if and when a state is faced with a law defining death, the following principles should be kept in mind:

• Dying is an activity of a living person, and death is the state of a human cadaver. Decisions regarding the use or nonuse of measures to prolong life are substantively different from criteria indicating that death has occurred. A law defining when death occurs should not be considered a grant of permission or mandate for the nonuse of means to sustain life, even though the practical effect of such a definition may result in the cessation of extraordinary efforts to maintain life.

• Laws defining when death occurs deal with the death of a human being, not simply — as Capron and Kass (1972) emphasize — the cessation of vital functions or the death of cells, tissues or organs. This emphasis is especially important since some physicians are now arguing that when certain functions cease, the patient is reduced to a "chronic vegetative state." Human life exists in a human person, and the absence of certain qualities or the inability to perform certain functions does not reduce a human being to the animal level or to being nothing more than a "human vegetable."

• Although doctors may be primarily responsible for the verification that death has occurred, the decision concerning the use of extraordinary procedures to prolong life is not simply a medical decision, nor is it based simply on medical criteria. *Doe v. Bolton,* the 1973 Supreme Court decision declaring Georgia's abortion law unconstitutional, illustrates the danger of designating life-and-death decisions simply as medical judgments. The Court argued that the Georgia law was unconstitutional because it restricted the physician from exercising "his best clinical judgment in the light of all the attendant circumstances." In striking down the Georgia law, the Court proposed that the physician be allowed to "range farther afield whenever his medical judgment, properly and professionally exercised, so dictates and directs him." The Court further decreed "that the medical judgment may be exercised in the light of all factors — physical, emotional, psychological, familial and the woman's age — relevant to the well-being of the patient. All these factors may relate to health. This allows the attending physician the room he needs to make his best medical judgment." This reasoning of the Court springs from an unlimited and unrealistic confidence in medical science, and an assumption that physicians possess wisdom and powers of judgment somewhat superior to those of other persons. It also assumes a universally held ethical tradition that is demonstrably absent in the overall society as well as in the medical profession. In light of these factors, if laws defining death are to be enacted, they should be based on specific scientifically verifiable criteria, not on nebulous social, psychological and familial factors. Moreover, such laws should be tightly written and equitably applied, and the decisions of doctors should be open to professional and public scrutiny.

• In cases where transplantation of organs is anticipated, the judgment that death has occurred should be reached by two physicians examining the patient independently, and neither of these should be a member of the transplant team.

Capron and Kass have cited these and other principles in a slightly different fashion. They also propose what they consider a "model statute" to guide legislatures (see Appendix "A"). Although the Capron-Kass formulation is an improvement on the Kansas statute, legislatures should be urged to move slowly and with great caution in regard to laws defining when death occurs.

Death with Dignity

These laws are customarily proposed to allow patients — and doctors and hospitals — to discontinue the use of extraordinary means for prolonging life when health can no longer be restored and when nothing other than the sustaining of vital processes is likely to be achieved. The common elements of "death with dignity" legislative bills are:

• A provision that there is no need to use extraordinary means to sustain life when death is imminent and health cannot likely be restored.

• A provision that there is no need to sustain life processes when health or functioning cannot be restored.

• A provision that gives a patient the prerogative to sign a document (usually called a Living Will) giving legal permission to discontinue extraordinary means.

• A provision that allows for proxy consent by the family or a committee of doctors.

Although the initial stated purpose of "death with dignity" laws is to allow people to determine in advance that extraordinary means need not be utilized when they are terminally ill, such laws are also perceived as the first step toward legally accepted mercy killing. One of the common elements of such laws is the Living Will, whereby a person signifies that extraordinary procedures need not be called upon to sustain life in certain circumstances. Behind the stated purpose is the expectation that the Living Will will condition the thinking of people to accept positive termination of life in cases of senility or incurable illness. Since 1967, the Euthanasia Educational Fund has conducted an intensive public information effort to persuade people to adopt a Living Will, regardless of legal requirements. Undoubtedly, the existence of such a document can give the physician a measure of encouragement to take positive steps to end life.

Indeed, in 1975 three state legislatures — those of Hawaii, Montana and Wisconsin — had bills introduced that envisioned active euthanasia. In the Montana proposal, for example, the word "euthanasia" is defined as the "painless inducement of death," and the bill further provides that euthanasia can be "administered" by a physician, a nurse, or by a family member or relative under the supervision of a physician (see Appendix "C").

The bill introduced in the state of Washington in 1975 reached to the matter of coercion. A physician or medical facility that opposes the implementation of the provisions of the Living Will "*shall have the duty* to make any necessary arrangements to effect the transfer of a qualified patient" (emphasis added) to medical personnel and facilities that will cooperate (see Appendix "C").

Worth or Lack of Worth of a Human Life

Perhaps most important of all, the euthanasia bills open the door to the legislative definition of the worth or lack of worth of a human life. The Delaware proposal (see Appendix "D") specifies that the life of the person who signs the Living Will "shall not be prolonged beyond the point of a *meaningful existence*" (emphasis added) (Sec. 1, par. 602[a]). In the Hawaii proposal (H. 342) the "irremediable condition" that justifies the administration of death is defined as a serious physical illness that is judged incurable and that either is "*expected* to cause him [the patient] severe *distress*" or "render him incapable of *rational existence*" (emphasis added) Sec. 3 [3]). The criteria of "meaningful" or "rational" existence or "distress" are quite vague and for that reason alone invite serious abuse.

In order to understand the full import of "death with dignity" bills, the efforts of Dr. Walter Sackett, sponsor and promoter of Florida's proposed statute, are instructive. Dr. Sackett, a member of the Florida legislature, has repeatedly introduced bills allowing euthanasia, and his intention is to use the legislative process to "educate" and "persuade" people to endorse "death with dignity" laws. Testifying before a U.S. Senate Committee on Aging (August 7, 1972) Dr. Sackett claimed that "death with dignity" laws are necessary because so many sick people wish to die, but are prevented from doing so due to physicians' fear of lawsuits for withdrawing treatment in the face of impending death. He also contended that money devoted to the special care required to keep severely retarded or disabled persons alive could be better spent on other medical problems.

It is worth noting that the Florida Association for Retarded Children condemned the Sackett bill as one that proposed "the intentional ending of life of persons who are disabled, physically and/or mentally, and who are limited in their ability to function." The association called on the National Association for Retarded Children "to repudiate publicly on a national scale, the proposed law and the philosophy which gives rise to it" (Resolution of the Florida Association for Retarded Children, September 15, 1973). On November 2, 1973, the National Association for Retarded Children responded positively to this request with a strongly worded resolution condemning the Florida bill and stating its opposition to all similar bills in other states.

At any rate, a major element of each proposed bill is the Living Will, which Dr. Sackett sees as the first step toward a "major change in American laws." Following close behind will be permission for next of kin to execute the Living Will. And finally, the permission of two doctors to execute the Living Will will suffice — at which point we can expect a shift in criteria from compassion for the patient to socio-economic justifications.

Nonetheless, Dr. Lawrence Foye, a cancer specialist with the Veterans Administration, also testified before the U.S. Senate Committee on Aging, and Dr. Foye argued that "the majority of critically ill persons do not have pain, and those that do can be controlled by the judicious use of pain-killing medicine." Dr. Foye also testified that in nine years of treating incurably ill cancer patients, he never had a patient who refused treatment or requested that he be allowed to die. Moreover, Dr. Foye rejected the approach of the Living Will because it is based on the false assumption that doctors can tell with certainty when the patient's condition is hopeless. Dr. Foye claimed that doctors cannot be certain when further treatment will be useless, and a Living Will signed years in advance supplies little help.

Officials of the Catholic Hospital Association (CHA) have expressed opposition to a legally sanctioned Living Will. In order to help people prepare for death and dying in a positive and Christian manner, the CHA Board of Directors, in June 1974, approved the "Christian Affirmation of Life." It is not intended as a legal document, nor is it expected to be used as such. Rather, it is a statement of Christian principles and attitudes in regard to death and dying.

At present, the American Medical Association remains opposed to "death with dignity" laws and to legislation defining death, considering it unnecessary and possibly harmful.

Moralists and ethicists generally do not favor establishing "death with dignity" laws since such laws are a poor approach to solving the human dilemmas of dying persons and their families. Moreover, attempts to deal with death within the narrow parameters of a legal definition generally ignore the far-reaching responsibilities that society has to protect human life and to provide care and compassion for each member of the human family in a manner consistent with human dignity. A law defining death and supplying minimal safeguards for protecting human life ignores the fact that death remains something of a mystery and that each person's dying is something of a loss to the entire human community.

Conclusion

In summary then, "death with dignity" laws are generally vague and ambiguous, and are neither necessary nor useful. In fact, they are often proposed as a first step toward legally permissible positive euthanasia.

Laws defining death are still a subject of controversy — enjoying the support of the American Bar Association and meriting rejection by the American Medical Association. In light of recent court cases, efforts to pass such laws will increase and may become a practical necessity. However, the formulation of such laws should be approached with caution, and every effort should be made to insure clarity of expression and intent.

Appendix 'A'

Definition of Death (1975 Legislative Report)

Traditionally the state legislatures meet on a biennial basis and for a limited period of time in the first months of the year. The current trend is toward annual sessions on a year-round basis.

To facilitate their work, legislatures often allow bills that were not fully acted on in one session to be carried over for further consideration the following year.

As of 1974 at least four state legislatures had enacted new definition-of-death laws: Kansas, 1970 (Ch. 378); Maryland, 1972 (Ch. 693); Virginia, 1973 (Ch. 252); California, 1974 (Ch. 1524). In 1975 three additional states enacted such laws: Illinois (Public Act 79-952), Oregon (Ch. 565), and Michigan (Public Act No. 158).

The actual wording of the new proposed definitions of death can vary considerably (different models are sometimes followed, e.g., the American Bar Association definition — these are noted below). But in general the new definitions propose that cessation of brain function be entered as a new and separate criterion for death, with great variation in the specific definition of brain death and in the conditions attendant on the determination of death.

By 1974 the Uniform Anatomical Gift Act, proposed by the National Conference of Commissioners on Uniform State Laws in 1968, had been adopted by virtually all the states. This act does not define death. It leaves the determination of death to the physician. "The time of death shall be determined by a physician who tends the donor at his death, or, if none, the physician who certifies the death. The physician shall not participate in the procedures for removing or transplanting a part" (Sec. 7 [b]).

STATE	BILL NO.	REMARKS	ACTION
Connecticut	S. 1350	ABA definition[1]	No action
Illinois	H. 1369	ABA defnition[1]	Enacted into law (Public Act 79-952)
Louisiana	H. 1470	Capron/Kass proposal[2]	Not enacted (amended, but died on House floor)
Michigan	H. 4653	Similar to Capron/Kass proposal[3]	Enacted into law (Public Act No. 158)
New	S. 3314		No action
Jersey	S. 3409		No action
New	S. 6243*		No action
York	S. 7860*		Reached Assembly floor where it was eventually recommitted to committee
Ohio	H. 1112*		No action
Oregon	H. 2648		Enacted into law (Ch. 565)
Pennsylvania	H. 363*	Similar to Kansas statute enacted 1970 (Ch. 378)	No action

*Bill carried over to the 1976 session.

1. The American Bar Association (ABA) definition reads: "For all legal purposes, a human body with irreversible cessation of total brain function, according to usual and customary standards of medical practice, shall be considered dead" (resolution adopted February 24, 1975). It is customary for such ABA definitions to be forwarded to the commission of Uniform State Laws as a basis for drafting a recommended bill. However, the American Medical Association is on record in opposition to a statutory definition of death (resolutions 1973, 1974 and earlier).

2. "A person will be considered dead if in the announced opinion of a physician, based on ordinary standards of medical practice, he has experienced an irreversible cessation of spontaneous respiratory and circulatory functions. In the event that artificial means of support preclude a determination that these functions have ceased, a person will be considered dead if in the announced opinion of a physician, based on ordinary standards of medical practice, he has experienced an irreversible cessation of spontaneous brain functions. Death will have occurred at the time when the relevant functions ceased." Capron, Alexander Morgan and Kass, Leon R., "A Statutory Definition of the Standards for Determining Human Death: An Appraisal and a Proposal," *University of Pennsylvania Law Review,* Vol. 121 (1972), 111.

3. See Appendix "B" for text.

Appendix 'B'

Definition of Death Laws
(Selected Texts)

The materials that follow are for purposes of illustration. They include the relevant sections of the three new laws enacted in 1975 — those of Illinois, Michigan and Oregon — as well as the first law enacted by the state of Kansas in 1970 (the laws of Maryland, Virginia and California are not included).

Kansas

[1970 — Ch. 378; effective July 1]

Definition of death. A person will be considered medically and legally dead if, in the opinion of a physician, based on ordinary standards of medical practice, there is the absence of spontaneous respiratory and cardiac function and, because of the disease or condition which caused, directly or indirectly, these functions to cease, or because of the passage of time since these functions ceased, attempts at resuscitation are considered hopeless; and, in this event, death will have occurred at the time these functions ceased; or . . .

A person will be considered medically and legally dead if, in the opinion of a physician, based on ordinary standards of medical practice, there is the absence of spontaneous brain function; and if based on ordinary standards of medical practice, during reasonable attempts to either maintain or restore spontaneous circulatory or respiratory function in the absence of aforesaid brain function, it appears that further attempts at resuscitation or supportive maintenance will not succeed, death will have occurred at the time when these conditions first coincide. Death is to be pronounced before artificial means of supporting respiratory and circulatory function are terminated and before any vital organ is removed for purposes of transplantation.

These alternative definitions of death are to be utilized for all purposes in this state, including the trials of civil and criminal cases, any laws to the contrary notwithstanding.

(Source: Kansas Statutes Annotated 1975 Supplement 77-202.)

Illinois

[1975 — Public Act 79-952; approved September 11; amends Sec. 2 of the Uniform Anatomical Gift Act; approved September 11, 1969, with respect to the definition of death]

"Death" means (for the purposes of the Uniform Anatomical Gift Act) the irreversible cessation of total brain function, according to usual and customary standards of medical practice.

Michigan

[1975 — Public Act No. 158; approved July 14; amends act providing for registration of births, deaths and adoptions, adding new section, Michigan Compiled Laws Annotated (MCLA) 326. 8b]

Section 8b (1) A person will be considered dead if in the announced opinion of a physician, based on ordinary standards of medical practice in the community, there is the irreversible cessation of spontaneous respiratory and circulatory functions. If artificial means of support preclude a determination that these functions have ceased, a person will be considered dead if in the announced opinion of a physician, based on ordinary standards of medical practice in the community, there is the irreversible cessation of spontaneous brain functions. Death will have occurred at the time when the relevant functions ceased.

(2) Death is to be pronounced before artificial means of supporting respiratory and circulatory functions are terminated.

(3) The means of determining death in subsection (1) shall be used for all purposes in this state, including the trials of civil and criminal cases.

Oregon

[1975 — Ch. 565; approved July 2]

Section I. In addition to criteria customarily used by a person to determine death, when a physician licensed to practice medicine under ORS, chapter 677, acts to determine that a person is dead, he may make such a determination if irreversible cessation of spontaneous respiration and circulatory function or irreversible cessation of spontaneous brain function exists.

Appendix 'C'

Euthanasia
(1975 Legislative Report)

Euthanasia bills were first introduced in state legislatures in the late 1930s, patterned after similar efforts in Great Britain. Euthanasia-related proposals have been appearing again in state legislatures in increasing numbers since the late 1960s.

No state has yet enacted a typical "death with dignity" bill into law. Most of these proposals envision passive euthanasia, but in 1975 proposals were introduced in three states — Hawaii, Montana and Wisconsin — that would allow active or positive euthanasia.

Preliminary reports show that in 1976 there were at least twenty states with euthanasia-related measures pending before them, the largest number of states ever. Euthanasia proposals were carried over from the 1975 to the 1976 sessions in seven states, and, in 1976 new proposals were introduced in at least thirteen other states: Alaska, Arizona, California, Florida, Georgia, Kentucky, Massachusetts, Minnesota, Missouri, New Jersey, Ohio, Tennessee and Virginia.

The United States Senate held hearings on "death with dignity" in 1972. In 1973, a bill was introduced in the U.S. House of Representatives (H.R. 2655) proposing a study commission on "death with dignity."

STATE	BILL NO.	CONTENT	ACTION
Delaware	H.30*	Death with dignity	No action
Florida	H. 239	Death with dignity	Not enacted (amended in subcommittee, but reported unfavorably by full Judiciary Committee)
Hawaii	SCR. 42*	Study commission	No action
	H. 342*	Death with dignity[1] (active euthanasia)	No action
Idaho	H. 95	Death with dignity	No action
Illinois	H. 11	Death with dignity	Not enacted (reported unfavorably, and then tabled)
	H. 618	Death with dignity	Not enacted (amended and reported favorably from committee, but defeated in full House)
Iowa	S. 207*	Death with dignity	No action
Maryland	S. 596	Death with dignity	Not enacted (hearings held)
	H. 764	Death with dignity	Not enacted (hearings held)
Massachusetts	H. 2297	Death with dignity	Not enacted (reported unfavorably by committee; subsequently twice substituted as study commission proposal [H. 5947 as substitute for H. 2297, H. 6043 as substitute for H. 5947]; the House ultimately rejected the study proposal [May 14])
Montana	H. 256	Death with dignity[2] (active enthanasia)	Not enacted (defeated in committee)
Nevada	SJR. 37	Memorial to Congress to pass a constitutional amendment to prohibit euthanasia (active and passive)	No action
New York	S. 6087*	Study commission on family life (including import of euthanasia, abortion, no-fault divorce, ERA, etc.)	No action
Rhode Island	H. 5196*	Death with dignity	No action
	H. 6512*	Study commission	No action
Virginia	H. 1595	Death with dignity	Not enacted (referred to subcommittee for further study)
Washington	S. 2881*	Death with dignity[3]	No action
Wisconsin	A. 1207*	Right to die[4] (active euthanasia)	No action

(See next page for explanatory notes.)

*Bill will be carried over to the 1976 session.

1. Death with dignity is defined as "the painless inducement of death" (Sec. 3 [2]), that is, the bill envisions active or positive euthanasia. The bill proposes conditions according to which a physician, or a nurse under a physician's direction, "administers death with dignity" (Secs. 8, 9).

2. The word "euthanasia" is defined as the "painless inducement of death" (Sec. 4 [2]), that is, the bill envisions positive or active euthanasia. Euthanasia can be "administered" by a physician, or by a nurse, family member or relative under the supervision of a physician (Sec. 8).

3. A physician or medical facility that opposed the implementation of the provisions of the Living Will *"shall have the duty* to make any necessary arrangements to effect the transfer of a qualified patient" to a physician or medical facility that will cooperate (emphasis added) (Sec. 8 [4]).

4. The bill creates a "right to die." Except as otherwise provided in this section, any person may request any person fourteen years of age or older to terminate the life of the requestor" (Sec. 1 [1]). The bill specifies a few conditions. A person under seven cannot make such a request. The request need only be made orally. The proposal in no way restricts itself to a medical context (but clearly encompasses it). For any reason whatever any person, who is seven years of age or older, can make a legally acceptable request of any other person, who is at least fourteen years of age, to kill him or her.

Appendix 'D'

Euthanasia
(Legislative Proposal)

The proposed euthanasia bills that have been introduced assume a variety of actual forms — some are more specific than others; some include a text for a Living Will and others do not, etc. Only the key elements of the 1975 Delaware bill are listed here, but this text illustrates the basic kinds of matter that euthanasia bills generally encompass.

DELAWARE

[House Bill No. 30 — introduced January 16, 1975; proposes to amend the Delaware Code by adding a new Chapter entitled "Death with Dignity"]

§601. *Definitions*

As used in this Chapter, unless otherwise provided or the context requires a different meaning:

"Terminal illness" means any illness that would result in natural expiration of life regardless of the use or discontinuance of medical treatment to sustain the life processes.

§602. *Death with Dignity*

(a) Any person, with the same formalities as required by law for the execution of a last will and testament, may execute a document directing that he shall have the right to die with dignity, and that his life shall not be prolonged beyond the point of a meaningful existence.

(b) In the event any person is unable to make such a decision because of mental or physical incapacity, a spouse or person or persons of first degree kinship shall be allowed to make such a decision, provided written consent is obtained from:

> (1)   The spouse or person of first degree kinship; or
>
> (2)   In the event of two (2) persons of first degree kinship, both such persons; or
>
> (3)   In the event of three (3) or more persons of first degree kinship, the majority of those persons.

(c) If any person is disabled and there is no kinship as provided in paragraph (b) of this section, death with dignity shall be granted any person if in the opinion of three (3) physicians the prolongation of life is meaningless.

§603. *Revocation of authorization to terminate sustaining medical treatment*

A person who has executed a document to refuse medical treatment under the provisions of §602(a) shall have the power to revoke said document at any time by oral or written statement; provided, however, that such revocation shall be witnessed by two persons.

§604. *Immunity for physicians*

A physician who relies on a document to refuse medical treatment or who makes a determination of terminal illness shall be presumed to be acting in good faith and, unless negligent, shall be immune from civil or criminal liability that otherwise might be incurred.

§605. *Filing of document*

Copies of any document executed under the provisions of this act shall be filed with the following: Prothonotary's Office in the respective county in which the person resides; the State Medical Examiner and Vital Statistics of the Division of Public Health.

Appendix 'E'

The Prolongation of Life
(An Address of Pope Pius XII to an International
Congress of Anesthesiologists)

Dr. Bruno Haid, chief of the anesthesia section at the surgery clinic of the University of Innsbruck, has submitted to Us three questions on medical morals treating the subject known as "resuscitation" [*la réanimation*].

We are pleased, gentlemen, to grant this request, which shows your great awareness of professional duties, and your will to solve in the light of the principles of the Gospel the delicate problems that confront you.

Problems of Anesthesiology

According to Dr. Haid's statement, modern anesthesiology deals not only with problems of analgesia and anesthesia properly so-called, but also with those of "resuscitation." This is the name given in medicine, and especially in anesthesiology, to the technique which makes possible the remedying of certain occurrences which seriously threaten human life, especially asphyxia, which formerly, when modern anesthetizing equipment was not yet available, would stop the heartbeat and bring about death in a few minutes. The task of the anesthesiologist has therefore extended to acute respiratory difficulties, provoked by strangulation or by open wounds of the chest. The anesthesiologist intervenes to prevent asphyxia resulting from the internal obstruction of breathing passages by the contents of the stomach or by drowning, to remedy total or partial respiratory paralysis in cases of serious tetanus, of polio-myelitis, of poisoning by gas, sedatives, or alcoholic intox-ication, or even in cases of paralysis of the central respira-tory apparatus caused by serious trauma of the brain.

The Practice of 'Resuscitation'

In the practice of resuscitation and in the treatment of persons who have suffered head wounds, and sometimes in the case of persons who have undergone brain surgery or of those who have suffered trauma of the brain through anoxia and remain in a state of deep unconsciousness, there arise a number of questions that concern medical morality and involve the principles of the philosophy of nature even more than those of analgesia.

It happens at times — as in the aforementioned cases of accidents and illnesses, the treatment of which offers reasonable hope of success — that the anesthesiologist can improve the general condition of patients who suffer from a serious lesion of the brain and whose situation at first might seem desperate. He restores breathing either through manual intervention or with the help of special in-struments, clears the breathing passages, and provides for the artificial feeding of the patient.

Thanks to this treatment, and especially through the administration of oxygen by means of artificial respiration, a failing blood circulation picks up again and the appear-ance of the patient improves, sometimes very quickly, to such an extent that the anesthesiologist himself, or any other doctor who, trusting his experience, would have given up all hope, maintains a slight hope that spontane-ous breathing will be restored. The family usually consid-ers this improvement an astonishing result and is grateful to the doctor.

If the lesion of the brain is so serious that the patient will very probably, and even most certainly, not survive, the anesthesiologist is then led to ask himself the distressing question as to the value and meaning of the resuscitation processes. As an immediate measure he will apply artificial respiration by intubation and by aspiration of the respiratory tract; he is then in a safer position and has more time to decide what further must be done. But he can find himself in a delicate position, if the family considers that the efforts he has taken are improper and opposes them. In most cases this situation arises, not at the beginning of resuscitation attempts, but when the patient's condition, after a slight improvement at first, remains stationary and it becomes clear that only automatic artificial respiration is keeping him alive. The question then arises if one must, or if one can, continue the resuscitation process despite the fact that the soul may already have left the body.

The solution to this problem, already difficult in itself, becomes even more difficult when the family [members] — themselves Catholic perhaps — insist that the doctor in charge, especially the anesthesiologist, remove the artificial respiration apparatus in order to allow the patient, who is already virtually dead, to pass away in peace.

A Fundamental Problem

Out of this situation there arises a question that is fundamental from the point of view of religion and the philosophy of nature. When, according to Christian faith, has death occurred in patients on whom modern methods of resuscitation have been used? Is Extreme Unction [Anointing of the Sick] valid, at least as long as one can perceive heartbeats, even if the vital functions properly so-called have already disappeared, and if life depends only on the functioning of the artificial-respiration apparatus?

Three Questions

The problems that arise in the modern practice of resuscitation can therefore be formulated in three questions:

First, does one have the right, or is one even under the obligation, to use modern artificial-respiration equipment in all cases, even those which, in the doctor's judgment, are completely hopeless?

Second, does one have the right, or is one under obligation, to remove the artificial-respiration apparatus when, after several days, the state of deep unconsciousness does not improve if, when it is removed, blood circulation will stop within a few minutes? What must be done in this case if the family of the patient, who has already received the last sacraments, urges the doctor to remove the apparatus? Is Extreme Unction still valid at this time?

Third, must a patient plunged into unconsciousness through central paralysis, but whose life — that is to say, blood circulation — is maintained through artificial respiration, and in whom there is no improvement after several days, be considered *"de facto"* or even *"de jure"* dead? Must one not wait for blood circulation to stop, in spite of the artificial respiration, before considering him dead?

Basic Principles

We shall willingly answer these three questions. But before examining them We would like to set forth the principles that will allow formulation of the answer.

Natural reason and Christian morals say that man (and whoever is entrusted with the task of taking care of his fellowman) has the right and the duty in case of serious illness to take the necessary treatment for the preservation of life and health. This duty that one has toward himself, toward God, toward the human community, and in most cases toward certain determined persons, derives from well-ordered charity, from submission to the Creator, from social justice and even from strict justice, as well as from devotion toward one's family.

But normally one is held to use only ordinary means — according to circumstances of persons, places, times, and culture — that is to say, means that do not involve any grave burden for oneself or another. A more strict obligation would be too burdensome for most men and would render the attainment of the higher, more important good too difficult. Life, health, all temporal activities are in fact subordinated to spiritual ends. On the other hand, one is not forbidden to take more than the strictly necessary steps to preserve life and health, as long as he does not fail in some more serious duty.

Administration of the Sacraments

Where the administration of sacraments to an unconscious man is concerned, the answer is drawn from the doctrine and practice of the Church which, for its part, follows the Lord's will as its rule of action. Sacraments are meant, by virtue of divine institution, for men of this world who are in the course of their earthly life, and, except for baptism itself, presuppose prior baptism of the recipient. He who is not a man, who is not yet a man, or is no longer a man, cannot receive the sacraments. Furthermore, if someone expresses his refusal, the sacraments cannot be administered to him against his will. God compels no one to accept sacramental grace.

When it is not known whether a person fulfills the necessary conditions for valid reception of the sacraments, an effort must be made to solve the doubt. If this effort fails, the sacrament will be conferred under at least a tacit condition (with the phrase *"Si capax est,"* "If you are capable," — which is the broadest condition). Sacraments are instituted by Christ for men in order to save their souls. Therefore, in cases of extreme necessity, the Church tries extreme solutions in order to give man sacramental grace and assistance.

The Fact of Death

The question of the fact of death and that of verifying the fact itself *("de facto")* or its legal authenticity *("de jure")* have, because of their consequences, even in the field of morals and of religion, an even greater importance. What We have just said about the presupposed essential elements for the valid reception of a sacrament has shown this. But the importance of the question extends also to effects in matters of inheritance, marriage and matrimonial processes, benefices (vacancy of a benefice), and to many other questions of private and social life.

It remains for the doctor, and especially the anesthesiologist, to give a clear and precise definition of "death" and the "moment of death" of a patient who passes away in a state of unconsciousness. Here one can accept the usual concept of complete and final separation of the soul from the body; but in practice one must take into account the lack of precision of the terms "body" and "separation." One can put aside the possibility of a person being buried alive, for removal of the artificial respiration apparatus must necessarily bring about stoppage of blood circulation and therefore death within a few minutes.

In case of insoluble doubt, one can resort to presumptions of law and of fact. In general, it will be necessary to presume that life remains, because there is involved here a fundamental right received from the Creator, and it is necessary to prove with certainty that it has been lost.

We shall now pass to the solution of the particular questions.

A Doctor's Rights and Duties

1. Does the anesthesiologist have the right, or is he bound, in all cases of deep unconsciousness, even in those that are considered to be completely hopeless in the opinion of the competent doctor, to use modern artificial-respiration apparatus, even against the will of the family?

In ordinary cases one will grant that the anesthesiologist has the right to act in this manner, but he is not bound to do so, unless this becomes the only way of fulfilling another certain moral duty.

The rights and duties of the doctor are correlative to those of the patient. The doctor, in fact, has no separate or independent right where the patient is concerned. In general he can take action only if the patient explicitly or implicitly, directly or indirectly, gives him permission. The technique of resuscitation which concerns us here does not contain anything immoral in itself. Therefore the patient, if he were capable of making a personal decision, could lawfully use it and, consequently, give the doctor permission to use it. On the other hand, since these forms of treatment go beyond the ordinary means to which one is bound, it cannot be held that there is an obligation to use them nor, consequently, that one is bound to give the doctor permission to use them.

The rights and duties of the family depend in general upon the presumed will of the unconscious patient if he is of age and *"sui juris."* Where the proper and independent duty of the family is concerned, they are usually bound only to the use of ordinary means.

Consequently, if it appears that the attempt at resuscitation constitutes in reality such a burden for the family that one cannot in all conscience impose it upon them, they can lawfully insist that the doctor should discontinue these attempts, and the doctor can lawfully comply. There is not involved here a case of direct disposal of the life of the patient, nor of euthanasia in any way: this would never be licit. Even when it causes the arrest of circulation, the interruption of attempts at resuscitation is never more than an indirect cause of the cessation of life, and one must apply in this case the principle of double effect and of *"voluntarium in causa."*

2. We have, therefore, already answered the second question in essence: "Can the doctor remove the artificial-respiration apparatus before the blood circulation has come to a complete stop? Can he do this, at least, when the patient has already received Extreme Unction? Is this Extreme Unction valid when it is administered at the moment when circulation ceases, or even after?"

We must give an affirmative answer to the first part of this question, as We have already explained. If Extreme Unction has not yet been administered, one must seek to prolong respiration until this has been done. But as far as concerns the validity of Extreme Unction at the moment when blood circulation stops completely or even after this moment, it is impossible to answer "yes" or "no."

If, as in the opinion of doctors, this complete cessation of circulation means a sure separation of the soul from the body, even if particular organs go on functioning, Extreme Unction would certainly not be valid, for the recipient would certainly not be a man anymore. And this is an indispensable condition for the reception of the sacraments.

If, on the other hand, doctors are of the opinion that

the separation of the soul from the body is doubtful, and that this doubt cannot be solved, the validity of Extreme Unction is also doubtful. But, applying her usual rules: "The sacraments are for men" and "in case of extreme necessity one tries extreme measures"; the Church allows the sacrament to be administered conditionally in respect to the sacramental sign.

When Is One 'Dead'?

3. "When the blood circulation and the life of a patient who is deeply unconscious because of a central paralysis are maintained only through artificial respiration, and no improvement is noted after a few days, at what time does the Catholic Church consider the patient "dead," or when must he be declared dead according to natural law (questions *de facto* and *de jure*)?"

(Has death already occurred after grave trauma of the brain, which has provoked deep unconsciousness and central breathing paralysis, the fatal consequences of which have nevertheless been retarded by artificial respiration? Or does it occur, according to the present opinion of doctors, only when there is complete arrest of circulation despite prolonged artificial respiration?)

Where the verification of the fact in particular cases is concerned, the answer cannot be deduced from any religious and moral principle and, under this aspect, does not fall within the competence of the Church. Until an answer can be given, the question must remain open. But considerations of a general nature allow Us to believe that human life continues for as long as its vital functions — distinguished from the simple life of organs — manifest themselves spontaneously or even with the help of artificial processes. A great number of these cases are the object of insoluble doubt, and must be dealt with according to the presumptions of law and of fact of which We have spoken.

May these explanations guide you and enlighten you when you must solve delicate questions arising in the practice of your profession. As a token of divine favors which We call upon you and all those who are dear to you, We heartily grant you Our Apostolic Blessing.

Reported in *L'Osservatore Romano,* November 25-26, 1957. French text. Translation based on one released by N.C.W.C. News Service.
This is a response to three questions submitted to the Holy Father by Dr. Bruno Haid, chief of the anesthesia section at the surgery clinic of the University of Innsbruck. It was delivered during an audience granted delegates to an International Congress of Anesthesiologists, meeting at Rome's Mendel Institute.

Selected Bibliography

Ad Hoc Committee of the Harvard Medical School to Examine the Definition of Brain Death. "A Definition of Irreversible Coma." *The Journal of American Medical Assocation,* Vol. 205 (Aug. 5, 1968).

Baylor Law Review. "Symposium Issue — Euthanasia." Vol. 27, No. 1, Winter, 1975.

Behnke, John and Sissela Bok, eds. *The Dilemmas of Euthanasia.* N.Y.: Doubleday, 1975. [Contains selected articles on euthanasia, and the text of the Harvard Report on Irreversible Coma.]

Branson, Roy. "Another Look at Elizabeth Kübler-Ross." *Christian Century,* 7 May 1975, pp. 464-468.

Brim, Orville G., and others, eds. *The Dying Patient.* N.Y.: Russell Sage Foundation, 1970. [Distributed by: Basic Books, P.O. Box 4100, Scranton, Pa. 18501. Cost: $10.]

Capron, Alex. "Determining Death: Do We Need a Statute?" *Hastings Center Report,* Feb. 1973.

————. and Kass, L. "A Statutory Definition of the Standards for Determining Human Death: An Appraisal and a Proposal." *University of Pennsylvania Law Review,* Vol. 121 (Nov. 1972).

Cutler, Donald B., ed. *Updating Life & Death.* Boston: Beacon Press, 1968. [Contains the Harvard Report on Irreversible Coma, and a commentary by Paul Ramsey.]

Death with Dignity: An Inquiry into Related Public Issues. Hearings before the Special Committee on Aging,

U.S. Senate, Aug. 7, 1972. Part I (44 pp.). Washington, D.C.: U.S. Government Printing Office. [Stock No. 5270-01632. Cost: 30¢. (Includes testimony of Rep. Walter Sackett endorsing a recommendation to allow ninety percent of 1,500 severely retarded children in Florida state hospitals to die.)]

Dedek, John. *Contemporary Medical Ethics.* N.Y.: Sheed and Ward, 1975.

Duff, Raymond S. and A. G. M. Campbell. "Moral and Ethical Dilemmas in the Special-Care Nursery." *New England Journal of Medicine,* Oct. 25, 1973, pp. 890-94. [Over a two-and-a-half-year period in a special-care nursery, forty-three infants suffering from serious congenital disorders, were allowed to die.]

Dyck, Arthur J. "An Alternative to the Ethic of Euthanasia." *To Live and to Die: When, Why and How.* Edited by Robert Williams. N.Y.: Springer-Verlag, 1973, pp. 98-112. [An ethical examination of euthanasia legislative proposals.]

Ethical and Religious Directives for Catholic Health Facilities. Washington, D.C.: Dept. of Health Affairs, United States Catholic Conference, 1971.

Euthanasia: Legislative Packet. Compiled by Bishops' Committee for Pro-Life Activities, 1312 Massachusetts Ave., N.W., Washington, D.C. 20005. [Copies of select euthanasia bills introduced into state legislatures in recent years. Cost: $3.]

"Facing Death." *Hastings Center Studies,* Vol. 2, No. 2, May 1974. Hastings-on-Hudson, N.Y.: The Hastings Center. [A compilation of essays on death, euthanasia and death with dignity, authored by Paul Ramsey, Robert S. Morison, Leon Kass and others.]

Feifel, Herman, ed. *The Meaning of Death.* N.Y.: McGraw Hill, 1959.

Ford, J. Massyngberde. *A Hospital Prayerbook*. Paramus, N.J.: Paulist Press, 1975.

Godin, Andre. *Death and Presence: The Psychology of Death and the Afterlife,* Vol. 3. Brussels: Lumen Vitae, 1971. Printed as a monograph In 1972. [Agent: Lumen Vitae, Aquinas Subscription Agency, 718 Pelham Blvd., St. Paul, Minn. 55114.]

Gould, J. and Lord Craigmyle. *Your Death Warrant?* New Rochelle, N.Y.: Arlington House, 1971. [Contains a history of euthanasia legislation in England, as well as substantive arguments against such laws.]

Graham, Robert A. "The 'Right to Kill' in the Third Reich: Prelude to Genocide." *Catholic Historical Review,* Jan. 1976. [An account of the Roman Catholic Church's opposition to the euthanasia programs of the Nazis directed at the German people.]

Greinacher, Norbert, and Alois Muller, eds. *The Experience of Dying.* N.Y.: Concilium No. 94, Herder and Herder, 1974. [Distributed by Seabury Press, 815 2nd Ave., New York, N.Y. 10017.]

Grollman, Earl A., ed. *Concerning Death: A Practical Guide for the Living.* Boston: Beacon Press, 1974.

Häring, Bernard. *Medical Ethics.* Notre Dame, Ind.: Fides, 1973.

Kesey, Ken. *Can They Defend Themselves?* Reprint No. 102, Right to Life League of Southern California, 301 S. Kingsley Dr., Los Angeles, Calif. 90020. [The noted modern novelist speaks out in defense of all life, regardless of its condition.]

Kübler-Ross, Elizabeth. *Questions and Answers on Death and Dying.* N.Y.: Macmillan, 1974.

————. *On Death and Dying.* N.Y.: Macmillan, 1969.

Kübler-Ross, Elizabeth, ed., *Death: The Final Stage of Growth.* Englewood Cliffs, N.J.: Prentice-Hall, 1975.

Linacre Quarterly. Journal of the National Federation of Catholic Physicians' Guilds, Vol. 42, Nos. 3, 4 (May 1975 and Aug. 1975). [Entire issues.]

Louisell, David. "Euthanasia and Biathanasia: On Dying and Killing." *Linacre Quarterly,* Nov. 1973.

Marx, Rev. Paul. *Death Without Dignity: Killing for Mercy.* Minneapolis, Minn.: For Life, Inc. (1917 Xerxes Ave.), 1975.

Morison, Robert. "Death: Process or Event." *Science,* Vol. 173, Aug. 20, 1971. [This issue of *Science* also carries a response by Leon Kass, "Death as an Event: A Commentary on Robert Morison."]

Morris, Arval A. "Voluntary Euthanasia." *Washington Law Review,* Vol. 15, No. 2, 1970, pp. 239-271. [An exploration of the thesis that death "is a mere matter of timing." Includes the text of a Voluntary Euthanasia Bill that has been proposed for introduction into the Washington state legislature.]

Nowell, Robert. *What a Modern Catholic Believes about Death.* Chicago: Thomas More, 1972.

O'Rourke, Rev. Kevin D., O.P. "Christian Affirmation of Life." *Hospital Progress,* July 1974, pp. 65-68.

Pincus, Lily, *Death and the Family.* N.Y.: Pantheon Books, 1974.

Ramsey, Paul. *The Patient as Person.* New Haven, Conn.: Yale University Press, 1970. [Contains a comprehensive moral analysis of euthanasia, of the use of ordinary and extraordinary means for preserving life, and of moral responsibilities toward the dying.]

Reynolds, Brad. "The Eerie Need to Redefine Death." *America,* Sept. 27, 1975.

Rizzo, Robert and Joseph Yonder. "Definition and Criteria of Clinical Death." *Linacre Quarterly,* Nov. 1973.

_____. "On Redefining Death." *America,* Feb. 14, 1976, pp. 122-23. [A response to Brad Reynolds' article, "The Eerie Need to Redefine Death" cited above.]

St. John-Stevas, Norman. "Euthanasia: A Pleasant Sounding Word." *America,* May 31, 1975, pp. 421-22.

Steinfels, Peter, ed. *Death Inside Out.* N.Y.: Harper Forum Paperback, 1975.

Task Force on Death and Dying, Institute of Society, Ethics, and the Life Sciences. "Refinements in Criteria for the Determination of Death: An Appraisal." *Journal of the American Medical Association,* Vol. 221, July 3, 1972.

Veach, Robert. "Brain Death: Welcome Definition or Dangerous Judgement?" *Hastings Center Report,* Nov. 1972.

_____. *Death and Dying.* Chicago: Claretian Publications, 1971. [Pamphlet. An excellent aid for families who are suffering with a dying member of any age.]

Villot, Jean Cardinal, Papal Secretary of State. Letter dated Oct. 3, 1970, to Dr. James Farrugia, secretary general of the International Federation of Catholic Medical Associations. [In the name of Pope Paul VI, Cardinal Villot called upon Catholic doctors to help set the standards in the area of medical ethics, and noted that every human life must be unconditionally respected.]

Wertham, Frederic, M.D. "The Geranium in the Window: the Euthanasia Murders." *A Sign for Cain: An Exploration of Human Violence.* N.Y.: Paperback Library, 1966. pp. 150-186. [Documents how the medical profession in Nazi Germany employed a "life devoid of value" ethic to justify the mass destruction of Germany's mentally ill, its crippled children and its old.]

Williams, Robert, ed. *To Live and To Die: When, Why and*

How. N.Y.: Springer-Verlag, 1973. [Contains a number of essays on death and euthanasia, including notable contributions by Arthur Dyck, Elizabeth Kübler-Ross, Joseph Fletcher.]

Wilson, Jerry. *Death by Decision.* Philadelphia: Westminster Press, 1975. [Attempts to set a framework for moral decision-making; accepts active euthanasia in certain circumstances.]

Selected Film Resources

All the Way Home. B/W. Films Inc., 440 Park Ave. So., New York, N.Y. 10016. Rental: $55 [Full-length film version of James Agee's "A Death in the Family."]

An Occurrence at Owl Creek Bridge. 27 min., B/W. Mass Media Ministries, 2116 N. Charles St., Baltimore, Md. 21218. Rental: $17.50. [Viewers are caught up into what it means to face death.]

Death. B/W. Filmmakers Library, 290 W. End Ave., New York, N.Y. 10023. Rental: $35. [Terminal illness of a fifty-two-year-old man filmed at Calvary Hospital, Bronx, N.Y.]

Those Who Mourn. 5 min., B/W and color. Teleketics, Franciscan Communications Center, 1229 S. Santee St., Los Angeles, Calif. 90015. Rental: $10; purchase: $80 (Cat. No. 8120). [Through memory flashbacks, the film explores the death of one man and its meaning to his wife.]

To Die Today. B/W. Filmmakers Library, 290 W. End Ave., New York, N.Y. 10023. Rental: $35. [Dr. Elizabeth Kübler-Ross lectures on the stages of dying, and, with medical students, interviews a terminal patient.]

Who Should Survive? Color. Mr. Herbert Kramer, Lowengard & Brotherhood, 999 Asylum Ave., Hartford, Conn. 06105. Rental: $20. [Reenactment of the famous Johns Hopkins case in which a defective newborn is permitted to die. Panel discussion follows.]

THE I TATTI
RENAISSANCE LIBRARY

James Hankins, General Editor

VALLA

ON THE DONATION
OF CONSTANTINE

LORENZO VALLA
❖ ❖ ❖
ON THE DONATION
OF CONSTANTINE

TRANSLATED BY

G. W. BOWERSOCK

THE I TATTI RENAISSANCE LIBRARY
HARVARD UNIVERSITY PRESS
CAMBRIDGE, MASSACHUSETTS
LONDON, ENGLAND
2008

Series design by Dean Bornstein

Library of Congress Cataloging-in-Publication Data

Valla, Lorenzo, 1407–1457.
[De falso credita et ementita Constantini donatione declamatio.
English]
On the donation of Constantine / Lorenzo Valla;
translated by G. W. Bowersock.
p.   cm. — (The I Tatti Renaissance library)
Originally published:
Cambridge, Mass.: Harvard University Press, 2007.
Without the Latin text.
Includes bibliographical references (p.   ) and index.
ISBN 978-0-674-03089-3 (pbk. : alk. paper)
1. Constitutum Constantini.   2. Popes — Temporal power —
Early works to 1800.   I. Bowersock, G. W. (Glen Warren), 1936–
II. Title.
BX875.D7V3413 2008
262'.132 — dc22   2008016361

Contents

卐

Introduction

꙳꙳꙳

Between 2 April and 25 May of the year 1440 Lorenzo Valla composed his devastating exposure of the so-called Donation of Constantine. His work refers explicitly to the death of the monstrous Cardinal Vitelleschi on 2 April. On 25 May Valla wrote a letter to his friend Giovanni Tortelli to accompany a copy of his recently completed *opusculum*.[1] The Donation provided the papacy, at least since the eighth century when it seems to have been fabricated, with a justification for its claims to political authority over the realms of the western Mediterranean. The document, allegedly written by Constantine the Great shortly before his death at Nicomedia in May 337, presented Pope Sylvester with title to the western part of his empire.

Until the early fifteenth century Constantine himself, considered as the author of the Donation, had been held personally responsible for the corruption of the temporal power of the popes,[2] but not long before Valla the Donation had come under fire in a treatise by Nicholas of Cusa,[3] and it must have figured importantly in the protracted debates about papal authority in the Councils of Ferrara and Florence in 1438 and 1439. The invalidation of the Donation should have meant that the corruption of the papacy could be conveniently postdated, to the advantage of Constantine's posthumous reputation, to the time when the forgery was made, but in fact his reign continued to figure as what Robert Black has called "a crucial turning point in history."[4]

Valla launched his assault on the authenticity of this document from his post as secretary to Alfonso, King of Aragon and Sicily, as the king was trying to wrest control of Naples from papal clients in the house of Anjou. Valla had himself sought an appointment from Pope Eugenius in 1431 and 1434, but without success.

He found a patron who appreciated him in Alfonso, who culti-
vated a circle of literary men in his entourage. Valla had already
proven himself a master of Latin style and the ancient classics,
with previous studies of Cicero and Quintilian, as well as a philosophical treatise on pleasure that was revised under the title of *On
the True Good*.

Valla's attack on the Donation is more reasonably seen as an ex-
tension of his literary and philosophical interests than as a political weapon offered to Alfonso in the struggle with Eugenius.
These were dangerous times, with the insecurity of Eugenius in Italy and the threat from the Ottoman Turks to the very existence
of Byzantine orthodoxy in the East. The Patriarch of Constantinople came to Ferrara and Florence in search of allies, and even
the Grand Prince of Moscow sent a representative of the Slavic
church. The validity of the Donation was hardly a new topic in
1440.

What was new was Valla's way of treating it. He split his work
into two main parts, rhetorical and philological. The opening part,
imagined as set in a court of kings and princes, brings together the
sons of Constantine, an orator representing the Roman senate and
people, and Pope Sylvester as petitioners before the jurors, and
they deliver elaborate speeches all designed to demonstrate the in-
herent implausibility of Constantine's giving away half his empire.
In the second part Valla rips apart the Latinity of the text of the
Donation to prove, brilliantly and decisively, that Constantine
could not have written it. His analysis of language and style has
often been seen, rightly, as the beginning of serious philological
criticism. His heirs, in acumen and savagery, were Richard Bentley
and A. E. Housman.

The speeches and the argument against the Donation are finely
spun with all the finesse of a master rhetorician.[5] Ultimately philology proves to be an even more powerful instrument than rhetoric for demolishing the document. But Valla makes no attempt to

develop a case for the other side, in favor of the Donation. For this reason alone it would be wrong to consider Valla's work a declamation, which, by the classic standard of Quintilian, should argue both sides of an issue. In his printed editions from the early sixteenth century Ulrich von Hutten first attached the title *Declamatio* to Valla's piece. Valla himself had never used it.

In his letter to Tortelli Valla wrote of his *opusculum* as concerned with canon law and theology, but in opposition to all canon lawyers and all theologians (*rem canonici iuris et theologie, sed contra omnes canonistas atque omnes theologos*).[6] This is not an unreasonable description since it is devoted to a document appended to the *Decretum* of Gratian, which constitutes the principal part of the fundamental corpus of canon law, and its theological implications for the papacy flow naturally from that.[7] Three years later, in a letter to his Greek teacher Giovanni Aurispa, Valla called his work a speech that was more rhetorical than anything he had written (*oratio qua nihil magis oratorium scripsi*).[8] It is evident that the work is presented as an *oratio*. It is full of addresses to putative listeners, while rhetorical questions and exclamations abound. Valla even conducts his detailed linguistic analysis in the form of a debate with the presumed forger, and at the end he launches a tirade addressed directly to the popes.

Although by the late sixteenth century Valla's fierce attack on the Donation and on the papacy itself seemed nothing less than incendiary and warranted placing the work on the Index of Prohibited Books in 1559,[9] it clearly did not look like that when it was written. It joined a debate that was already current at the time, especially after a repudiation of the document in 1433 by Nicholas of Cusa.[10] Soon after the *oratio* appeared in 1440 the humanist Gregorio Tifernate, who was a colleague of Valla's at the court of Alfonso, read it and proclaimed that it had been written *pro Christi ecclesia, non contra ecclesiam* — in support of the church of Christ, not against the church.[11]

By late 1443, however, two cardinals, Trevisan and Landriani, appear to have made some effort to persuade Valla to retract or revise his work, possibly with a view to satisfying his longstanding desire to return to Rome. We have only Valla's side of the correspondence, but it could not be clearer about Valla's intentions. In fact, in November 1443, writing to Trevisan, he himself put the question, "Why did I write *On the Donation of Constantine?*" He would have preferred to have written the work under another pope than Eugenius. The defense of truth and the conviction of falsehood were his sole objectives. He could not suppress or emend the work even if he had to, and even if he could he would not feel that he had to.[12] To Landriani in January 1444 Valla acknowledged that he had stirred up enemies at Rome as a result of his *oratio*, but, were it not for his mother who lived there, he attached no importance to their threats.[13]

Curiously, after Valla's correspondence with the two cardinals in late 1443 and early 1444, there is no trace of any interest in his work on the Donation until copies dating from the 1480s. Although Valla's enemies in Eugenius' entourage managed to bring him before the Inquisition at Naples in 1444, the accusations turned entirely on his other writings and, so far as can be told, had nothing to do with the Donation. They arose from his criticism of Aristotle and Boethius. Alfonso, who had already won his claim to Naples through a treaty with the pope at Terracina in June of the previous year, succeeded in closing down the investigation against Valla. In 1448, after Eugenius' death, the next pope, Nicholas V, finally made Valla apostolic *scriptor* in Rome, and in 1455 Calixtus III named him papal secretary. Apart from personal enmity in the court of Eugenius there was no sign that the papacy was smarting from his demolition of the Donation.

Notoriety lay in the future. Copies of Valla's *oratio* from the late fifteenth century provided the basis for a little noticed and now very rare printed edition, the first ever, in 1506. But when Ulrich

von Hutten printed the text twice in successive years, in 1518 and 1519, it spawned reprints of the original Latin as well as translations into modern European languages. By 1546 it was available in Czech, French, German, English, and Italian. Its value for reformation theology was immediately apparent, and it soon became an embarrassment for a church that had accepted it with equanimity a century before. Luther famously hailed it soon after von Hutten had made it widely available. Later no less a personage than Cardinal Baronius denounced it in a strenuous defense of the Donation. Baronius even went so far as to invoke brickstamps that he claimed to have seen when the original basilica of St. Peter's was taken down to make way for Michelangelo's creation at the Vatican. He reported that the brickstamps named Constantine himself, and these were advanced as proof of Constantine's support of the papacy. But we now know that Baronius deliberately falsified what he saw in an effort to shore up papal claims to Constantinian support.[14] Although the spirit of Lorenzo Valla can rest in peace today, the Catholic church still inveighs against him for loose morals and licentiousness.[15]

It is difficult to approach his *opusculum* without being reminded of its later notoriety. Yet, read on its own terms, it is immensely rewarding simply as a bravura exercise in rhetoric and philology. Keeping company with Valla is a thrilling experience. His writing evokes a powerful mind fueled by dazzling erudition. His mastery of the Latin language makes most of his contemporaries look like barbarians, as he would have been the first to assert. To summon up an English voice for so great a writer, without burdening him with antiquarian diction that would traduce him by alienating him, is formidably difficult. The strength of his arguments for the implausibility of the Donation and the incisiveness of his philological dissection of its Latin text must come through without destroying the pulsating energy of his prose.

To pepper the translation with Latin words in parentheses would perhaps make the translation more serviceable for those who are trying to negotiate the original, but it would drain the text of all its blood and leave a cold cadaver where there had once been flaming passion. For example, Valla mocks the diction of the forger by observing that in the course of his inflated language he pretentiously uses *extat* for *est, nempe* for *scilicet,* and *concubitores* for *contubernales.* It would seriously diminish the impact of Valla's outrage if all these Latin words were inserted into the text of the translation. But an English equivalent may be offered as follows:

> Everything is stuffed with these words — *we decree, we adorn, imperial, imperatorial, power, glory;* and he has put *exists* in place of "is," since existing implies prominence or superiority, and *indeed* for "of course," and *bed-mates* for "companions." Bed-mates are those who sleep together and have intercourse, and must naturally be understood to be whores.

Similarly, when the forger made Constantine order that the holy clergy should ride on horses adorned with white saddles, he wrote *ut clerici sancti . . . equos equitent.* In his excellent English translation of 1922, Christopher Coleman hit upon precisely the right equivalent, *that the holy clergy . . . should mount mounts.*[16] Not every English equivalent can be so stylishly felicitous, but an anglophone reader deserves to have the best approximation possible.

The depth and range of Valla's reading is astonishing. He quotes freely from Scripture and always from memory, as slight variations in the order of words or verses clearly demonstrate. Similarly, in drawing examples from Latin and Greek authors of classical antiquity, he plucks apposite lines at will from such voluminous writers as Livy, Valerius Maximus, Macrobius, and Homer. He clearly knew Virgil's *Aeneid* by heart and could produce phrases and whole lines effortlessly. His knowledge of Hebrew surfaces in a brief but accurate discussion of the name

Kephas in the New Testament. With a few deft strokes he evokes institutions and titles from the history of republican and imperial Rome. His treatment of the relative social status of senator and patrician is exceptionally acute, and his knowledge of provincial organization under Constantine allows him to highlight grotesque anachronisms. The most egregious of these is the forger's use of the term "satraps" to refer to high-ranking officials.

It is now generally agreed that the forgery was made in the middle to late eighth century. Johannes Fried has recently explored its historical context as well as the significance of its espousal in the Middle Ages. He sees Frankish opposition to the emperor Louis the Pious as the background for the original fabrication.[17] The manuscript tradition, as sorted out by Horst Fuhrmann in his edition of the document, which is known as the *Constitutum Constantini*,[18] reveals extensive alteration and editing by copyists over succeeding centuries. Comparison of Valla's text with the one established by Fuhrmann shows that he was in possession of a considerably improved text through Gratian, even though quite enough barbarisms remained for him to destroy it with his sharp philological instruments.

Curiously, historians of Rome now know, as Valla did not, that the subscription at the end of the document, providing a date in the joint consulship of Constantine (for the fourth time) and a certain Gallicanus, indicts the forger unequivocally.[19] The consular list, as scholars can reconstruct it today from various testimonia, reveals that Constantine and Gallicanus never served in the same year. Constantine was consul in 329, Gallicanus in 330. Furthermore, in 329, although the consul Constantine was serving for the fourth time, this was not the emperor but his son. In that year the emperor was consul for the eighth time. Let this revelation be offered admiringly here to the shade of Lorenzo Valla.

For someone coming to the *oratio* on the Donation for the first time, there could be no better salutation than the words of

Apuleius at the opening of his novel, *Metamorphoses* or *The Golden Ass: Lector intende, laetaberis* — Reader, pay attention, you will enjoy it!

NOTES

1. For the circumstances of composition and the *Nachleben* of Valla's work, the fundamental study remains W. Setz, *Lorenzo Vallas Schrift gegen die Konstantinische Schenkung*, Bibliothek des Deutschen Historischen Instituts in Rom 44 (Tübingen, 1975). The preface to Setz's edition of the work in the *Monumenta Germaniae Historica, Quellen zu Geistesgeschichte des Mittelalters* vol. 10 (Weimar, 1976), resumes the fundamental points about composition and provides a list of manuscripts and printed editions. The less said the better about the deplorable edition of Walther Schwahn (Leipzig, 1928), on which see Setz's preface, p. 46, n. 146. Teubner reprinted it in 1994.

2. See the richly documented account of the Donation in the Middle Ages in Robert Black, "The Donation of Constantine: A New Source for the Concept of the Renaissance," in *Languages and Images of Renaissance Italy*, ed. Alison Brown (Oxford, 1995), pp. 51–85, especially pp. 63–67 on the denunciations of Constantine by Marsilius of Padua, Dante, and Petrarch.

3. Cusanus attacked the treatise's authenticity in his *De concordantia catholica*, 3.2. See note 10 below.

4. Black, *op. cit.* (n. 2 above), pp. 70–71.

5. See Salvatore I. Camporeale, "Lorenzo Valla e il *De falso credita donatione*. Retorica, libertà ed ecclesiologia nel '400," *Memorie domenicane* n.s. 19 (1988), 191–293, and his summary treatment in "Lorenzo Valla's *Oratio* on the Pseudo-Donation of Constantine: Dissent and Innovation in Early Renaissance Humanism," *Journal of the History of Ideas* 57 (1996), 9–26.

6. *Laurentii Valle Epistole*, ed. O. Besomi and M. Regoliosi (Padua, 1984), no. 12, p. 192.

7. Valla knew well (and discusses at length) that the Donation was a later insertion into the Decretum of Gratian, and canonists had treated the document as suspect: Rudolf Weigand, "Fälschungen als Paleae im Dekret Gratians," in *Monumenta Germaniae Historica, Schriften,* Bd. 33. 11: *Fälschungen im Mittelalter,* Teil II (Hannover, 1998), pp. 301–318, with particular reference to the Donation on pp. 310–311. See also D. Maffei, *La Donazione di Costantino nei giuristi medievali* (Milan, 1964).

8. *Epistole* (n. 6 above), no. 23, p. 252.

9. Cf. Setz, *Lorenzo Vallas Schrift* (n. 1 above), pp. 100–101, 151–194, and Giovanni Antonazzi, *Lorenzo Valla e la polemica sulla Donazione di Costantino, con testi inediti dei secoli XV–XVII* (Rome, 1985).

10. See Riccardo Fubini, "Contestazioni quattrocentesche della Donazione di Costantino: Niccolò Cusano, Lorenzo Valla," in *Costantino il Grande dall' antichità all' umanesimo,* ed. G. Bonamente and F. Fusco (Macerata, 1992), 1: 385–431. Fubini returned to this topic in his paper, "Humanism and Truth: Valla Writes against the Donation of Constantine," in *Journal of the History of Ideas* 57 (1996), 79–86. He argued that Valla knew Cusanus' analysis in *De concordantia catholica,* and he surmised that this knowledge "might have been the very reason for his writing on the Donation of Constantine." Fubini's case for Valla's familiarity with Cusanus' argument, particularly in the domain of canon law, is strong.

11. *Epistole* (n. 6), no. 12a, p. 193.

12. *Epistole* (n. 6), no. 22, p. 247: *At cur De Constantini donatione composui? . . . Id ego tantum abest ut malivolentia fecerim, ut summopere optassem sub alio pontifice necesse mihi fuisse id facere, non sub Eugenio. . . . Opus meum conditum editumque est, quod emendare aut supprimere nec possem si deberem, nec deberem si possem. Ipsa rei veritas se tuebitur aut ipsa falsitas se coarguet.*

13. *Epistole* (n. 6), no. 25, p. 255: *Causam meam, ut opinor, nosti: de opere, inquam Constantiniane donationis, ob quod multis sancte apostolice sedis senatoribus invisus sum et reus agor, immo peragor ab inimicis meis atque invidis.* He says that he is reproached and terrorized for attacking the liv-

ing as well as the dead: *quam ego reprehensionem terroremque, nisi matris causa, que istic est, pro meo more nihil facerem.*

14. For proof, see the photograph on p. 10 of G. W. Bowersock, "Peter and Constantine," in *St. Peter's in the Vatican*, ed. W. Tronzo (Cambridge, 2005), with notes 36 and 38 on pp. 14–15.

15. See, for example, the article under his name in the current *Catholic Encyclopedia*.

16. Christopher B. Coleman, *The Treatise of Lorenzo Valla on the Donation of Constantine* (New Haven, 1922), p. 117. Jean-Baptiste Giard found an equally appropriate French rendering in his translation for the series *La roue à livres* (Paris, 1993), pp. 66 and 73: *que les saints clercs . . . chevauchent des chevaux.*

17. Johannes Fried, *"Donation of Constantine" and "Constitutum Constantini": The Misinterpretation of a Fiction and its Original Meaning*, with a contribution by Wolfram Brandes, "The Satraps of Constantine" (Berlin, forthcoming, 2007). For the intellectual context of Valla's work, Carlo Ginzburg, in his preface to the Giard translation (see the previous note), is worth reading.

18. See Fuhrmann's text, included in this volume, with a translation providing comparisons with Valla's quotations from the document.

19. For bibliography and details see the final note to the translated *Constitutum* in this volume. The view that the forger might have had the years 315 ot 317 in mind (cf. Camporeale, n. 5 above) presupposes a reference to Constantine's real fourth consulate or another Gallicanus. But such early dates, even for the forger, would be preposterous.

Acknowledgments

❦❦❦

I am greatly indebted to four learned friends for encouraging and supporting me in the preparation of this work. The first is James Hankins, editor of the I Tatti Renaissance Library. Knowing that I have long admired Valla's demolition of the Donation of Constantine, he made the somewhat improbable proposal that I translate the piece for his series. Since Valla's Latinity is at a very high standard, a classicist and ancient historian such as myself could feel comfortable with it. Professor Hankins' support, in general and in detail, has been indispensable. As both editor and bibliographer, he has greatly enriched this volume.

Second, Christopher Jones, my dear friend of close to fifty years and James Hankins' colleague in the Harvard History Department, has meticulously read through my entire translation as well as the introduction. With his sharp eye and impeccable Latin he led me to improve my text in more places than I can count. He too knew how much I appreciated Valla's *oratio*.

Third, the numismatist Jean-Baptiste Giard sent me his French translation of Valla's work, with a stimulating preface by Carlo Ginzburg, as soon as it appeared in 1993. This rekindled my interest, and it was perhaps the main reason why I allowed myself to be persuaded to write an iconoclastic paper on Constantine and St. Peter, in which I suggested that the initiative for the first Vatican basilica came from Constans.

Finally, the late and deeply missed John Shearman espoused my view of the Vatican basilica and offered me confirmatory evidence for it. As I persevered in my research on Constantine, my mind turned constantly to Valla, and in my introduction to the translation the reader will see traces of that encounter.

ON THE DONATION
OF CONSTANTINE

LORENZO VALLA
ON THE FORGED AND
MENDACIOUS DONATION OF
CONSTANTINE

Many, many books have issued from my pen in almost every   1
area of learning, and in these I have disagreed with some great authors of long established reputation. Inasmuch as there are those
who feel ill treated and accuse me of recklessness and impiety,
what must we imagine they are going to do now? How much will
they rant against me? And if they have the chance, how eagerly
and swiftly will they carry me off to punishment? I am one who
writes not only against the dead, but against the living as well—
not one or two of them, but many—and not merely against private persons but even against those who hold high office! What
office-holders they are! The supreme pontiff, of course, who is
armed not only with a temporal sword in the manner of kings and
princes, but an ecclesiastical one as well, so that you cannot find
protection from him by sheltering, so to speak, under the shield
of any prince, to avoid being struck down by excommunication,
anathema, or execration. If the man who said, *I am unwilling to
write against those who have the power to proscribe,*[1] should be thought
to have acted as prudently as he spoke, how much more should I
act similarly towards someone who does not even allow the possibility of proscription? And he would pursue me with the invisible
darts of his power, so that I could rightly say, *Whither shall I go
from your spirit, and whither shall I flee from your face?*[2] Unless by
chance we think that the supreme pontiff will bear these assaults
with greater tolerance than others would. Hardly, since Ananias,
the high priest, in the presence of the tribune who was sitting as
judge, ordered Paul to be struck on the mouth because he said

that he passed his life with a good conscience, and Phasur, holding
the same office, threw Jeremiah into prison for his outspokenness.
But the tribune and the governor had the power and the desire to
protect the former from priestly abuse, and the king the latter. Yet
what tribune, what governor, what king will be able, even if he
wishes, to snatch me from the hands of the supreme priest if he
seizes me?

2   But there is no reason why this double threat of danger should
trouble me or keep me from my plan. For the supreme pontiff is
not allowed to bind or release anyone contrary to human and divine law, and giving up one's life in the defense of truth and justice
is a mark of the greatest virtue, the greatest glory, the greatest reward. Many indeed have gone to the point of death to defend their
earthly fatherland: shall I be deterred by the threat of death for
striving to reach my heavenly fatherland, as do those who please
God, not men? Anxiety be gone, let fears retreat far away, and
worries disperse! With a bold spirit, great confidence, and good
hope, the cause of truth, the cause of justice, and the cause of God
must be defended. No one who knows how to speak well can be
considered a true orator unless he also dares to speak out. So let
us dare to accuse one who commits deeds that deserve accusation,
and let one who sins against all be reviled by the voice of one who
speaks for all. Yet perhaps I ought not to censure a brother openly
but *between ourselves:*[3] on the contrary a person who sins in public
and who accepts no private counsel must be charged in public, *to
frighten all the rest.*[4] Did not Paul, whose words I have just used,
reproach Peter to his face before the church, *because he was
reproachable,*[5] and leave this in writing for our instruction? But I
am not a Paul who can reproach a Peter: I am rather a Paul who
imitates Paul in such a way — which is something much greater —
as to become one spirit with God, since I scrupulously obey his
mandates. Personal status does not make anyone safe from attacks.
It did not do so for Peter and for many others endowed with the

same rank, such as Marcellus for pouring libations to the gods, — such as Celestinus for agreeing with the heretic Nestorius, — such as certain persons also in our own time, who we know were rebuked by persons of inferior status (who is *not* inferior to the Pope?), to say nothing of those who have been condemned.[6]

I am not acting to satisfy a desire to harass anyone and to write   3
Philippics against him — may I not be guilty of such a heinous deed —, but to eradicate error from people's minds, to remove persons from vices and crimes by admonition and reproof. I would not dare say that others, instructed by me, should prune with steel the papal seat — the vineyard of Christ — which is teeming with undergrowth, and force it to bear plump grapes instead of emaciated berries. When I do this, will there not be someone who would wish to stop my mouth or his own ears, to say nothing of calling down punishment and death? If so, even if it be the Pope himself, what kind of man should I say he is: a *good shepherd*, or a *deaf snake that would not hear the voice of the charmer*[7] and would prefer to go at the charmer's limbs with a poisonous bite?

I know that for a long time people have been waiting to hear
the accusation I would bring against the Roman pontiffs: a massive accusation assuredly, of either supine ignorance or monstrous avarice, which is enslavement to idols, or pride of rule, which is always accompanied by cruelty. Already for several centuries they either did not realize that Constantine's Donation was a lie and a fabrication, or else they invented it themselves. Their descendants, following the deceitful path of earlier generations, defended as true what they knew to be false — dishonoring the majesty of the pontificate, dishonoring the memory of the pontiffs of old, dishonoring the Christian religion, and confounding everything with slaughter, collapse, and crime. They say that the city of Rome is his, that the kingdom of Sicily and Naples is his, that the whole of Italy is his, the peoples of Gaul, Spain, Germany, and Britain, — in short that the West is his: they say that all these are encompassed

in that document of donation. Is all this yours because of that, supreme pontiff? Do you intend to recover all of it? Is it your idea to despoil of their cities all the kings and princes of the West and to force them to pay you annual tribute? I, on the contrary, think that the princes have a better right to despoil you of the entire empire you hold. For, as I shall show, that Donation, from which the supreme pontiffs want to derive their legal right, was unknown to Sylvester and Constantine alike.

5   But before I come to refuting the Donation document, which is the sole authority those people have, something that is not only false but even crude, structure demands that I go back farther. First, I shall assert that Constantine and Sylvester were not such men as, with the former, to want to make a donation, to be in a legal position to do so, and to have in his power the ability to hand over these territories to someone else, and, with the latter, to want to receive them and be in a legal position to do so. Second, even if these points were other than absolutely true and very clear, I shall assert that the one did not accept and the other did not hand over the possession of the things that are said to have been donated, but that they remained forever under the jurisdiction and authority of the Caesars. Third, I shall assert that nothing was given by Constantine to Sylvester, but rather to the previous pontiff before he received baptism, and that these were modest gifts of places where the Pope could spend his life. Fourth, I shall assert that it is falsely claimed a copy of the Donation was found among the emperor's decrees or was extracted from the Story of Sylvester, because it is neither found in that story nor in any other, and because in it are contained various contradictions, impossibilities, stupidities, barbarisms, and absurdities. Furthermore I shall speak about donations of certain other emperors — whether fictitious or worthless — and there I shall add from abundant evidence that if Sylvester ever had taken possession, once he or some other pontiff had been had been deprived of it, after so great an interval of time

it could not be recovered by any legal claim, human or divine. Lastly, I shall assert that the supreme pontiff's current possessions could not, in the course of time, have been administered under his authority.

: I :

To turn to the first part, we shall speak at the start about 6 Constantine, then about Sylvester. It is unacceptable to make a public and, so to say, imperial case with the same kind of presentation as normally accorded to private cases. Therefore I permit myself to plead as if in an assembly of kings and princes, into whose hands I am confident my speech will come, and to address them as if they were present in front of me.

I speak to you, kings and princes. Since it is hard for a private 7 person to form any idea of a royal disposition, I probe your mind, I examine your conscience, I ask for your testimony: Would any one of you, had he been in Constantine's place, have thought he should act to bestow upon another person, by gracious liberality, the city of Rome — his own fatherland, the center of the world, the queen of cities, the most powerful, noblest, richest of peoples, which triumphed over nations and was sacred to behold? Would he have thought to remove himself to a modest town, or after that to Byzantium,[8] and, in addition, to turn over Italy along with Rome, not just a province but a victor over provinces? Would he have thought to give away the three Gauls, the two Spains, the Germans, the British — the whole western world — and to deprive himself of one of the two eyes of his empire? I cannot be persuaded to believe that any sane person would do this. What is normally more desirable, more pleasurable, more welcome than for you to enlarge your empires and kingdoms and to extend your sway as far and wide as possible? It seems to me that all your con-

cern, all your thinking, all your effort is taken up day and night with this. From this arises your special hope of glory. Because of this you put aside worldly delights, because of this you submit to a thousand perils, because of this you give up with equanimity your loved ones and your own limbs. As far as I have heard or read, not one of you was ever deterred from the effort to increase his empire because he would have lost an eye, a hand, a leg, or some other member. On the contrary, this blazing passion for extensive rule most of all goads and drives one who is already supremely powerful. Alexander — who was not content to have wandered on foot through the deserts of Libya, to have subdued the East to the farthest sea, to have conquered the north amid a multitude of wounds and misfortunes, as his troops were already balking and were loathing such distant and rough campaigns — seemed to himself to have accomplished nothing at all without the subjugation of the West and all its nations either by force or by the authority of his name. Indeed, if he had already planned to explore and bring under his control the Ocean as well as any other world there might be, he would finally, in my opinion, have tried to scale heaven itself. Such is the desire of almost every king, even if not all kings share his audacity. I forbear to mention how many crimes, how many abominations have been committed in the cause of gaining or increasing empire, so that brothers do not hold back their evil hands from brothers' blood, nor sons from parents', nor parents from sons'. In no other endeavor does human recklessness normally assert itself so much and so fiercely. You may marvel when you see that in this the old are no less eagerly minded than the young, the childless no less than parents, kings no less than tyrants.

8   But if dominion is apt to be sought by so great an effort, how much greater must be the effort to keep it! Not enlarging an empire is not so wretched as reducing it. Even more grotesque than not adding another's realm to yours is allowing yours to be added

to another's. For when we read that persons have been placed in charge of a kingdom or of cities by some king or people, this did not concern the main or largest part of the empire, but some minor and insignificant part, with the aim of making the recipient forever acknowledge the donor as his master and himself as his servant.

Now I ask, do not those who think that Constantine gave away ⑨ the better part of his empire appear to be lowly and ignoble? I am not referring to Rome and Italy and the rest, but to the Gauls, where he himself had fought battles, where alone he had the dominion for a considerable time, where he had laid down the foundations of his glory and his empire. This was a man who launched wars on nations out of lust for rule; who had deprived allies and relatives of their empire after pursuing them in civil war; who had not yet subdued and dispatched the remains of the opposing faction; who not only was given to waging wars with many nations from hope of glory and empire but also considered it necessary inasmuch as he was assaulted daily by barbarians; who was rich in progeny, blood relations, and friendships; who knew that the Senate and People of Rome would fight against him; who had experienced the instability of conquered nations that rebelled almost every time there was a change of Roman emperor; who remembered, just like the other Caesars, that he had taken his rule not through senatorial election and consent of the plebs, but through an army, weapons, and war. What cause was so strong and pressing that he would neglect all these things and choose to manifest such liberality?

They say, "Because he had become a Christian." Would he ⑩ therefore give up the best part of his empire? To reign now was, I suppose, wicked, criminal, and impious, nor could his kingdom be conjoined with the Christian religion. Those who are adulterous, who enlarge their capital by usury, who possess what belongs to another normally give back, after baptism, someone else's wife,

money, or property. If you follow this line of thought, Constantine, you ought to give back freedom to the cities, not to change their master. But you say that was not the issue — you were moved to do all this in order to honor religion. As if it would be more religious to give up your realm than to administer it to safeguard religion! For as far as the recipients are concerned, that donation of yours will be neither respectable nor advantageous in their eyes. In fact, if you wish to show yourself a Christian, to demonstrate your piety, to provide for — I do not say the Roman church, but the church of God — you should now, now above all, play the prince, to fight for those who cannot and must not fight, to keep safe through your authority those who are subject to plots and injuries. God wanted the secret of truth to be made manifest to Nebuchadnezzar, Cyrus, Ahasuerus, and many other princes, and yet he demanded of none of them to withdraw from empire or to make a gift of part of his realm, but only to give back freedom to the Hebrews and to protect them from hostile neighbors. This was enough for the Jews. This will be enough for the Christians too. Did you become a Christian, Constantine? Yet it is most improper for you now as a Christian emperor to have a smaller dominion than you had as an unbeliever. Dominion is a certain special gift of God, for which even pagan princes are thought to be chosen by God.

11   "But he was cured of leprosy: therefore it is likely that he wanted to express his gratitude and to give back more than he had received." Really? When Naaman the Syrian was cured by Elisha he wanted to offer only gifts, not half his possessions. Would Constantine have offered half his empire? I regret that I am responding to a shameless tale as if it were irreproachable history, for this tale was concocted out of the history of Naaman and Elisha, as was a second tale, about a dragon, out of the mythical dragon of Bel. But granted all that — does any mention of the Donation occur in this history? By no means! But more on this later.

He was cured from leprosy and on that account adopted a   12
Christian disposition; he was suffused with the fear of God and
with the love of God. He wanted to hold Him in honor. Nevertheless, I cannot be persuaded that he wanted to give away so
much, since I see that no one, neither a pagan to honor his gods
nor a believer to honor the living God, has laid down an empire
and given it over to priests. In fact not one of the kings of Israel
could be induced to permit the people to go to Jerusalem to sacrifice, in the old way, at the temple, evidently out of fear that, moved
by that holy religious ritual and by the majesty of the temple, they
might perchance return to the king of Judah, from whom they had
rebelled. How much greater than this is what Constantine is said
to have done! And lest you delude yourself on account of the cure
of leprosy: Jeroboam was chosen first by God to be the king of Israel, and indeed from a lowly status — which in my opinion is
much more than being cured of leprosy —, yet he did not make
bold to entrust his kingdom to God. Do you want Constantine to
have donated to God a kingdom that he had not even received
from him? He would assuredly offend his sons (which did not
happen to Jeroboam), humiliate his friends, neglect his relatives,
damage his country, afflict everyone with grief, and be forgetful of
himself as well.

If he had been like that and, so to speak, turned into a different   13
person, there would certainly not have been lacking people to ad-
monish him, especially his sons, relatives, and friends. Is there
anyone who would not suppose that they would have gone to the
emperor straightaway? Imagine them trembling before your eyes,
once the intention of Constantine had been made known — hus-
tling, prostrating themselves with wailing and tears at the prince's
knees, and speaking as follows:

"Father, do you really deprive, disinherit, and cast off your   14
sons, you who loved your sons very much until now? We do not
so much bemoan as wonder at your desire to strip yourself of the

best and greatest part of your empire. But bemoan it we do, because you are transferring it to others at our expense and to our disgrace. What reason is there for you to cheat your children from the anticipated succession to your empire, when you yourself ruled together with your father? What have we done against you? In what way do we appear guilty of disrespect towards our fatherland, the name of Rome, and the majesty of her empire? The fairest and best part of the principate you strip away from us, who are banished from our ancestral homes, from the sight of our birthplace, from the air we used to breathe, and from our traditional way of life. Shall we as exiles abandon our hearths, our shrines, and our tombs to dwell in some unknown region of the earth? We are your kin, your friends, who have stood so often with you in the line of battle, who have watched our brothers, our parents, and our sons quivering when they were impaled on the point of an enemy sword. We were not terrified by another's death and were ready ourselves to meet death for you. Are all of us now deserted by you? We who hold magistracies at Rome, who govern or shall govern the cities of Italy, the Gauls, the Spains, and all the other provinces — are we all recalled, all ordered to be stripped of office? Or will you make up this loss from some other place? How will you be able to do this in a proper and worthy manner when so much of the world has been handed over to someone else? Surely, Caesar, you will not place a man who governed a hundred peoples in charge of only one? How could such an idea ever enter your mind? How did you suddenly become so forgetful of your own that you have no pity at all for your friends, none for your kinsmen, none for your sons? If only, Caesar, we had fallen in battle with your reputation intact and victory secure rather than look upon this! You can indeed do what you want with your empire and even with us, with one exception, which we will fiercely uphold unto death — we shall not desist from the worship of the immortal gods and shall serve as a great example to others, so that

you may know what your vaunted largesse does for the Christian religion. For if you do not bestow the empire upon Sylvester, we are willing to be Christians with you and many others will follow suit, but if you do bestow it, we will not only refuse to become Christians, but you will cause the very name of Christian to be hated, loathed, and cursed by us, and you will make us such that you will pity our life and death, and you will not blame us, but you yourself for being implacable."

Would not Constantine have been moved by this speech, if not 15 already moved on his own, unless we suppose that his humanity had been altogether rooted out of him? If he had been unwilling to listen to these men, were there not those who would oppose this action in both word and deed? Would the Senate and the Roman People have thought they should do nothing in such a situation? Would they not have summoned an orator who was, in Virgil's phrase, *respected for his goodness and his public service*,[9] to deliver the following speech before Constantine?

"Caesar, if you are unmindful of your own family and even of 16 yourself, so that you wish your sons to have no inheritance, your relatives no wealth, your friends no honors, and you no empire intact, nevertheless the Senate and People of Rome cannot be unmindful of its right and its reputation. For how can you arrogate to yourself so much of the Roman empire, which was brought forth from our blood, not yours? Will you cut one body into two parts, and will you make two realms out of one, two capitals, two wills? And will you offer to two brothers, as it were, the swords with which to decide their inheritance? To states which have served this city well we give the rights of citizenship, that they may be Roman citizens: are you taking away half of the empire from us to stop them recognizing this city as their own parent? Even in beehives, if two kings are born, we kill the one that is weaker: do you, in the hive of the Roman empire, where there is one outstanding leader, think that another should be installed,

who is weak in the extreme and not a bee but a drone? We greatly miss good sense on your part, Majesty. For what is going to happen if, either in your lifetime or after your death, a war is launched by barbarian nations upon this part that you are giving away or upon the other that you are keeping for yourself? Now, with the resources of the whole empire, we scarcely have the capacity to act: will we have it then? Will the one part be forever in harmony with the other? In my judgment this will be impossible: when Rome wishes to rule, the other part would be unwilling to be enslaved. In fact, as long as you are alive, once former governors have been recalled and new ones put in their place, when you have set out for your own kingdom and are far away while another rules here, will not everything be changed in a short time, in other words chaotic and contrary? Usually when a kingdom is divided between two brothers, the minds of the people are divided straightaway, and they expect war among themselves before responding to external enemies. Who does not see that the same will happen in this empire? Or are you unaware that formerly this was the principal reason why the aristocrats declared they would rather die in the sight of the Roman people than allow the passage of a measure that would have sent part of the Senate and part of the people to settle in Veii, and the establishment of two cities of the Roman people in common?[10] For if there was so much dissension in one city, what would there be in two cities? At this time, if there is so much strife in one empire — I call to witness your own knowledge and efforts —, what will happen in two empires? Come now, do you imagine that there would be anyone here who would either want to come to your aid when you are engaged in war or know how? Those who will be put in charge of soldiers and cities will be repelled by arms and warfare of all kinds, just like the one who appoints them. Tell me, will not the Roman legions or the provinces themselves attempt to despoil this man, so unskilled in ruling and so vulnerable to harm, as someone they will expect either not to

fight back or not to take revenge? I really believe that those appointees will not remain in their posts for even one month but will immediately rebel upon the first report of your departure. What will you do, what plan will you adopt, when you will be overwhelmed by two and even more wars? We can scarcely contain the nations that we have subjected: how will they be held back when war arises from free peoples?

"You, Caesar, will look after yourself, but this matter concerns 17 us just as much as you. You are mortal. The empire of the Roman people must be immortal and, insofar as lies with us, it will be — not only the empire but our sense of honor as well. But shall we accept an empire of those whose religion we scorn? And shall we, as princes of the world, be subservient to this most contemptible creature? When the city was captured by the Gauls the aged Romans refused to allow their beards to be stroked by the victors. Now will so many members of the senatorial order, so many praetorians, so many tribunicians, so many consulars and holders of triumphs tolerate the domination of those whom they themselves have treated as miscreant slaves with all manner of insults and punishments? Will those men set up magistracies, rule provinces, wage wars, impose capital penalties upon us? Will the Roman nobility go on campaign for them, hope for decorations, and gain rewards? What greater wound can we receive, what wound goes deeper? You should not imagine, Caesar, that Roman blood has so degenerated that it will tolerate that with equanimity and not think it should be avoided by whatever means — something, I have to say, our women would not endure. They would rather burn themselves up with their dear children and the gods they cherish at home, for the women of Carthage should not be stronger than those of Rome.

"Caesar, had we chosen you as king, you would indeed have 18 great control over the Roman empire, but not such that you could diminish its sovereignty in the slightest. On the contrary, we who

had made you king would have ordered you by the same process to give up your throne, so that you could not divide the kingdom, not give away so many provinces, not turn over the very capital of the kingdom to a foreigner of the lowliest kind. We put a dog to protect the sheep-pen, but if the dog prefers to play the role of a wolf we either get rid of it or kill it. Now, since you have played the dog's part for a long time in defending the Roman sheep-pen, will you at the last, without any precedent, be transformed into a wolf? And, since you force us to speak rather candidly in support of our right, you need to realize that you have no legal claim on the empire of the Roman people: Julius Caesar seized rule by force, Augustus took over the crime and made himself the ruler by wiping out the opposing factions. Tiberius, Gaius, Claudius, Nero, Galba, Otho, Vitellius, Vespasianus and all the rest plundered our freedom by the same or a similar route. You too became ruler after expelling or exterminating others, and I forbear to mention that you were an illegitimate child. Therefore, to make our mind known to you, Caesar, if you do not care to keep the government of Rome, you have sons, one of whom you may put in your place with our permission, and on our proposal, in accordance with the law of nature. Otherwise it is our intention to defend the public interest together with our own personal reputation. For this is no less an affront to the descendants of Romulus than was once the rape of Lucretia, nor will a Brutus be wanting to offer himself as a leader to this people against Tarquinius in the restoration of our freedom.[11] We will draw our swords first against those whom you put over us, then against you yourself, just as we have done against many emperors and for lesser reasons."

19   Certainly these points would have moved Constantine, unless we think he was made of stone or wood. If the people had not spoken out, it would still be imaginable that they spoke among themselves and raged in words like these.

Let us now move on and suppose that Constantine wanted to 20
gratify Sylvester, whom he would be subjecting to so many men's
hatred and swords that, as far as I can tell, Sylvester would
not have remained alive for a single day. For with him and a few
others out of the way, every hint of so terrible an outrage and insult would seem to have been removed from the breasts of the
Romans. But let us just suppose, if at all possible, that prayers,
threats, and any argument were unavailing and that Constantine
still persisted and refused to retreat from his decision, once he had
taken it. Who would not agree that he would have been moved at
Sylvester's speech, if there had really been one? Doubtless it would
have been like this:

"Caesar, my excellent liege and son, I cannot but cherish and 21
embrace your devout outpouring of piety, and yet I am not too
surprised that in offering gifts to God and in sacrificing victims
you stray somewhat into error, since you are still a recruit in the
Christian army. Just as formerly it was not proper for a priest to
sacrifice just any kind of cattle, wild animal, and bird, so too
should he not accept just any kind of gift. I am a priest and a
pontiff, who has to determine what I may allow as an offering at
the altar, to protect against the offering of an animal that is not
just impure but a viper or a snake. So consider this. Suppose
you had the right to hand over to someone other than your sons a
part of your empire containing Rome, the reigning capital of the
world — something I do not at all believe — ; suppose this people,
suppose Italy, suppose all the other nations, seduced as they are by
worldly attractions, would agree, against all plausibility, that they
preferred to be subject to those whom they hate and whose religion they have hitherto spat upon. Even so, my most loving son —
if you think you owe me some credence — I could still not be induced by any argument to agree with you unless I wished to be
untrue to myself, forget my station, and almost deny my Lord Je-

15

sus. Your gifts or, as you prefer, your remunerations would stain and immediately wipe out the glory, innocence, and sanctity of myself and of all those who will come after me, and they would block the way for those who will come *to know the truth*. Elisha was unwilling to accept a payment when Naaman the Syrian was cured of leprosy: shall I accept one when you have been cured? He repudiated gifts: shall I allow kingdoms to be given to me? He was unwilling to besmirch the role of prophet: shall I have the capacity to besmirch the role of Christ, which I take upon myself? Why did he think that the role of prophet was besmirched by receiving gifts? Surely because he could appear to be selling sacred commodities, making money off the gift of God, needing the protection of men, weakening and diminishing the merit of his benefaction. Consequently he preferred to make princes and kings his own beneficiaries rather than to be himself their beneficiary, and not even to enjoy mutual benefaction. *For it is much more blessed*, as the Lord said, *to give than to receive*. The same applies to me, only more so, since I am instructed by the Lord, saying, *Heal the sick, raise the dead, cleanse the lepers, drive out demons; freely have you received, freely give*. Shall I commit so great a crime, Caesar, as not to follow God's precepts, to stain my own glory? *It is better*, as Paul said, *for me to die than for anyone to take away my glory*. Our glory is to honor our ministry before God, as Paul also declared, *I say to you pagans, as long as I am the apostle of the pagans, I shall glorify my ministry*.[12] Should I be for others, Caesar, both an example and a cause of wrongdoing? I who am a Christian man, priest of God, Roman pontiff, vicar of Christ?

22   "How, moreover, will the blamelessness of priests remain secure amid wealth, magistracies, and the administration of secular business? Have we forsworn earthly things to such an extent that we pursue more opulent forms of the same things? Have we put aside our private property in order to possess the property of other peo-

ple as well as public property? Will cities belong to us, taxes, and levies? And if we do this, what right will we have to be called clergy? Our portion or lot, which is called *klēros* in Greek, is the Lord—it is not a terrestrial but a heavenly lot. The Levites, who were also clergy, were not allotted a portion with their brothers: do you bid us to be allotted even our brother's portion? What are wealth and riches to me? I am bidden by the voice of the Lord to take no care for tomorrow, and I have been told by him: *Do not build up treasure on earth, do not keep gold or silver or money in your wallets,* and: *It is more difficult for a rich man to enter the kingdom of heaven than for a camel to pass through the eye of a needle.* And so he chose the poor as his ministers and those who gave up everything to follow him. He was himself an example of poverty. To a great extent the handling of wealth and money is an assault on innocence, not only the possession and control of it. Judas alone, who had the purses and carried the alms that were put into them, was a liar and from love of money, to which he had become accustomed, reproached and betrayed his master, his Lord, his God. And so I fear, Caesar, that you may turn me from a Peter into a Judas. Hear also what Paul says: *We have brought nothing into this world, and there is no doubt that we can take nothing away from it. Having food and the wherewithal to cover ourselves let us be content. For those who want to become rich fall into temptation and into the devil's snare and into many useless and injurious desires, which plunge men into death and perdition. The root of all evils is greed, which some have espoused in leaving the faith and bringing upon themselves much pain. You, man of God, flee from these things.*[13] Do you, Caesar, bid me accept what I ought to avoid like poison?

"Furthermore, in your wisdom, Caesar, consider this: what   23
place will there be among all these things for doing God's work? The apostles replied to certain persons who complained that their widows were being neglected in the apostles' daily ministry that it

was not right for them to abandon the word of God and serve at tables. Yet how much different is serving at widows' tables from exacting taxes, managing the treasury, counting out soldiers' pay, and being involved in a thousand other responsibilities of this kind? *No warrior of God involves himself in worldly affairs,* said Paul.[14] Did Aaron, together with all the others of the race of Levites, attend to anything other than the tabernacle of God? His sons were consumed by a celestial fire because they put a foreign flame into their censers. And you are telling us to put the fire of worldly wealth — a fire forbidden and profane — into our holy censers, that is, into our priestly offices? Did Eleazar, Phineas, and all the other pontiffs and ministers of the tabernacle or temple administer anything that was unrelated to their divine office? I say "administer," but could they have administered anything if they wanted to do their duty? But if they should not want to do it, they would hear the execration of God saying: *Accursed are those who negligently perform the work of God.*[15] This execration falls not only upon everyone but particularly upon pontiffs. How great is the responsibility of the pontiff! What it is to be the head of the Church! What a great burden it is to be placed as a shepherd in charge of so great a flock. The blood of every single lamb and sheep that has been lost is upon his hand. To him it has been said: *If you love me more than others do, feed my lambs; again, if you love me as you say you do, feed my sheep; yet a third time, if you love me as you say you do, feed my sheep.*[16] Do you, Caesar, bid me also feed goats and pigs, who cannot be protected by the same shepherd?

24   "Tell me, do you want to make me a king or rather a Caesar — a ruler of kings? When the Lord Jesus Christ, God and man, king and priest, acknowledged that he was a king, listen to what he said about his kingdom: *My kingdom,* he said, *is not of this world. For if my kingdom were of this world, my ministers would assuredly fight back.*[17] What was the first thing he said, the often repeated pur-

port of his preaching? Was it not this? *Repent! The kingdom of heaven is approaching! The kingdom of God is approaching!*[18] To what will the kingdom of heaven be compared?[19] When he said these things, did he not declare that a secular realm had nothing to do with him? Not only did he not seek a kingdom of this kind: he was unwilling to accept one that was offered to him. For when he realized at one moment that peoples had in mind to take him away and make him a king, he fled into the wilderness of the mountains. This is what he gave to us who stand in his place, not only as an example to be imitated, but as a precept, when he said: *The princes of the pagans rule over them, and the greater ones use their authority against them. It will not be like that among you, but whoever should wish to become greater among you, let him be your servant, and whoever should wish to be the first among you shall be your slave — just as the Son of Man did not come to be served but to serve and to give his life to redeem many.*[20]

"In former times, as you know, Caesar, God set up judges, not kings, over Israel, and he abhorred the people for asking to have royalty. Because of the obstinacy in their hearts he gave them a king but only in such a way as to allow a rejection, which he revoked in a new law. Shall I accept a kingdom, when I am scarcely allowed to be a judge?[21] *Are you unaware,* said Paul, *that the saints will be judges over this world? If the world be judged among yourselves, it is beneath you to judge the smallest matters. Are you unaware that we shall judge the angels? How much more secular matters! If you have secular lawsuits, put forward as judges those who are lowliest in the church.*[22] And yet judges will adjudicate only controversial cases, not demand payment as well. Shall I demand one? I know that when Peter was asked by the Lord from whom the kings of the earth received tribute or tax, whether from their sons or from foreigners, He declared, when Peter answered "from foreigners," *Therefore their sons are free.*[23] But if all people are my sons, Caesar, as they surely are, all of them will be free, no one will pay anything. Therefore I have

25

no need of your donation, by which I would assume a task that it would be as wrong for me to bear as it is impossible.

26   "Why would I consider it necessary to have power over life and death, to punish the guilty, to wage wars, to destroy cities, to ravage territories by fire and sword? In no other way would I hope to be able to protect what you had transferred to me. And if I act in this way, am I a priest, a pontiff, the vicar of Christ? I should hear Him thundering against me and saying: *My house will be called the house of prayer for all peoples, and you have made it a robbers' cave. I did not come into the world, says the Lord, to judge the world, but to free it.*[24] Shall I, who am His successor, be a cause of deaths? I, to whom it was said in the person of Peter: *Put your sword back in its place, for all those who have taken a sword will perish by the sword.*[25] We are not even allowed to defend ourselves with a weapon—since Peter wanted to defend the Lord when he cut off the slave's ear.[26] Do you bid us employ a weapon for the acquisition or protection of riches? Our power is the power of the keys, as the Lord says: *I shall give you the keys of the kingdom of heaven. Whatever you bind on earth will be bound in heaven too, and whatever you let loose on earth will be loosed in heaven too. And the gates of Hell shall not prevail against them.*[27] Nothing can be added to this power, nothing to this rank, nothing to this kingdom. Whoever is not content with this is demanding something else for himself from the devil, who dared to say even to the Lord: *I shall give you all the kingdoms of the world, if you fall on the ground and worship me.*[28] Therefore, Caesar—allow me to say this without offense—do not play the devil for me, you who tell Christ, namely me, to accept kingdoms of the world that are given by you. I prefer to repudiate them than to possess them; and—to speak of unbelievers but, I hope, future believers—do not turn me from an angel of light into an angel of darkness for those whose hearts I want to draw into piety, whose necks I do not want to bring under the yoke. I want to subject them to myself *with the sword that is the word of God,*[29] not with a sword of iron, so

that they may not become worse, kick back, gore me, and, vexed by my error, blaspheme the name of God. I want to make them my dearest sons, not my slaves; to adopt them, not buy them; to father them, not subject them; to offer their souls as a sacrifice to God, not their bodies to the devil. *Learn from me*, the Lord said, *who am gentle and of a humble spirit. Take my yoke and you will find rest for your souls. For my yoke is agreeable and my burden light.*[30] Finally, to come to an end, on this matter hear that remark which He uttered as if directed to you and me: *Render to Caesar the things that are Caesar's, and to God the thing that are God's.*[31] Wherefore it turns out that neither you, Caesar, should give up what is yours nor should I accept what is Caesar's. Even if you should offer it a thousand times, I would never accept."

To this speech of Sylvester, worthy of an Apostle, what could 27 Constantine put forward in rebuttal? Under the circumstances, those who say that the donation was made — do they not damage Constantine by asserting that he wanted to deprive his own family and tear apart the Roman empire? Do they not damage the Senate and the Roman people, Italy and the entire West, which allowed, they say, the empire to be transformed, contrary to laws human and divine? Do they not damage Sylvester, who, they say, accepted a donation unworthy of a holy man? Do they not damage the supreme pontificate, which they imagine is allowed to control earthly realms and to manage the Roman empire? All these points serve to show that Constantine would never, as they claim, have acted in the face of so many obstacles to bestow the Roman state, in large part, upon Sylvester.

: II :

Let us move on. To believe in that donation, which your docu- 28 ment mentions, there has to be some evidence of Sylvester's accep-

tance. None now exists. "But," you say, "it is believable that he approved this donation." It is as believable, in my opinion, as that he not only approved it but even sought it, asked for it, and extorted it by his prayers. Why do you say that something that goes beyond human imagining is believable? We do not have to think that the donation was accepted just because the grant is mentioned in the document about the donation. On the contrary, we must say that the donation was never made because there is no mention of an acceptance. There is more evidence against you that Sylvester rejected the gift than that Constantine wanted to make it. *A benefaction cannot be bestowed upon someone who does not want it.*[32]

29   We ought to suppose that Sylvester not only repudiated the gifts but also indicated implicitly that Constantine had no right to bestow them and that he himself could not rightfully accept them. The blindness and injudiciousness of greed! Let us grant that you can also bring forward genuine documents — uncorrupt and authentic — concerning the agreement of Sylvester: whatever items were mentioned in those documents were not turned over straightaway, were they? Where is the possession of them? Where the transference of property? For if Constantine merely gave a piece of paper, he did not want to be nice to Sylvester but to make fun of him. "It is likely," you say, "that a donor is also the one who assigns possession." Look at what you are saying, since clearly possession was not granted and the question is whether a legal claim was. It is likely that whoever did not give possession did not want to give even a title.

30   Surely it is evident that possession was never granted — something it would be outrageous to deny? Did Constantine bring Sylvester to the Capitol, almost in triumph amid the applause of crowds of unbelieving Roman citizens? Did he place him upon the golden throne in the presence of the entire Senate? Did he order the magistrates, each in accord with his rank, to greet their king

and prostrate themselves before him? This normally happens for new emperors, not merely the transference of some such palace as the Lateran. Did Constantine take Sylvester on a tour of all Italy? Did he visit the Gauls with him, the Spaniards, the Germans, and all the western empire? Or if both of them were overwhelmed by such a circuit of territories, to whom did they entrust such a huge responsibility—persons who would give possession on the emperor's behalf and take it on Sylvester's? They had to have been great men of exceptional authority, and yet we do not know who they were. How weighty are those two words: give and take! Leaving aside examples from the ancient past, we have never, to the best of my knowledge, seen matters handled in any other way, when someone was made master of a city or a region or a province, than that possession is considered to be finally given over when former magistrates are removed and new ones put in their place. If Sylvester had not demanded at the time that this be done, it would nonetheless have been in the interest of Constantine's dignity to assert that he was giving over possession not only in word but in deed, that he was displacing his own governors and ordering others to be put in their place by Sylvester. There is no transfer of possession if it remains in the hands of the same persons who had it before, and the new master dares not remove them. But suppose that even this does not stand in the way, and we acknowledge that Sylvester is nevertheless deemed to have been in possession, and that everything was then managed in an untraditional and unnatural manner. After Constantine's withdrawal, to whom did Sylvester entrust the stewardship of provinces and cities? What wars did he wage? What nations on the verge of armed revolt did he suppress? Through what subordinates did he manage these things? "We do not know anything about this," you answer. So I imagine that everything was accomplished in the dead of night, and that is why no one saw anything.

31   All right, Sylvester had possession: Who deprived him of it?
For neither he nor any of his successors remained in possession in
perpetuity, at least down to Gregory the Great. Even he did not
have possession. Anyone who is not in possession and cannot
prove that he was dispossessed assuredly never had possession at
all and is delirious if he says that he had. You see that I am prov-
ing you too to be delirious if you cannot tell me who dispossessed
the Pope. Was it Constantine himself, or his sons, or Julian, or
some other emperor? Produce the name of the man who expelled
him, produce the date when he was first expelled, when for a second time, when after that. Was it through rebellion and slaughter,
or without these? Did nations conspire all together against him, or
which one came first? Tell me, did no one of all those peoples
come to help him, not even some of those whom Sylvester or
some other Pope had put in charge of the cities and provinces?
Did he lose absolutely everything on one day, or bit by bit over
time? Did he himself offer resistance along with his magistrates,
or did they abdicate at the first sign of trouble? Tell me, did not
the victors themselves move, sword in hand, against the dregs of
mankind they judged unworthy of empire to take vengeance for
insults, to take over the power that had been usurped, to trample
upon our religion, even to set an example for posterity? Did absolutely no one of those who were conquered take flight, go into hiding, or feel afraid? What an amazing episode! The Roman empire,
acquired with so much effort and with so much blood, was acquired or lost by Christian priests so calmly and so quietly that no
blood, no war, no contention intervened, and—what must be no
less amazing—no one at all knows by whom this was done, when,
how, and for how long. You would think that Sylvester ruled in
the woods among trees, not in Rome among men, and was expelled by winter rains and chills, not by people. Who is not aware,
if he has done a little serious reading, how many kings were ap-

pointed at Rome, how many consuls, how many dictators, how many tribunes of the plebs, how many aediles? No one escapes us from this large crowd of persons, from the most ancient of days. Similarly we know how many leaders of the Athenians there were, of the Thebans, of the Spartans, and we remember all their land and sea battles. We are not ignorant of the kings of the Persians, the Medes, the Chaldaeans, the Hebrews, and many others, and how each of these assumed his kingdom or retained it or lost it or recovered it. But of Sylvester's Roman empire it is not known, even in the city of Rome itself, in what way it began or ended, when, or through whom. I ask you: would you be able to produce any witnesses of these things or any writers about them? "No," you reply, and you, who are more cattle than people, feel no shame in saying that Sylvester probably had possession.

Since you are unable to do this, I, on the contrary, shall show 32 that down to the last day of his life Constantine had possession and so did all the emperors in succession after him, so as to leave you with nothing to sputter at. Yet it is exceedingly difficult, in my opinion, and very laborious to show this. Let all the Latin and Greek histories be spread out, let all other authors who have mentioned those times be cited, and you will discover that none is at variance with another in this matter. Let one out of a thousand testimonies suffice—Eutropius, who saw Constantine, who saw the three sons of Constantine left by their father as masters of the world, who wrote as follows about Julian, the son of Constantine's brother: *This Julian gained power and with a huge army waged war against the Parthians in an expedition in which I too participated.*[33] He would not have kept quiet about a donation of the western empire, nor a little later would he have said about Jovian, who succeeded Julian: *With Sapor he made a necessary peace but an ignoble one, with boundary changes as a consequence of giving up some part of the Roman empire—something that had never happened before from the time the Ro-*

man empire was founded. In fact our legions had been sent under the yoke at the Caudine Forks by Pontius Telesinus and in Spain at Numantia and in Numidia so that none of our territory should be given up.[34]

33   At this point I should like to turn to you, the most recent Roman popes (though you are now deceased), and to you, Eugene, who are still alive but only by the grace of Felix.[35] Why do you loudly proclaim the Donation of Constantine and frequently threaten certain kings and princes as if you were exacting vengeance for a purloined empire? And why do you squeeze out some sort of admission of subjection from the emperor when he has to be crowned, as well as from some other rulers, such as the King of Naples and Sicily—something that not one of the older Roman popes ever did, not Damasus with Theodosius, not Syricius with Arcadius, not Anastasius with Honorius, not John with Justinian, nor other very saintly popes with other excellent emperors? On the contrary, they always maintained that Rome and Italy, together with the provinces I have named, belonged to the emperors. For this reason gold coins, of which I own many specimens, were in circulation (I do not speak here of other monuments and shrines of the city of Rome), bearing an inscription in Latin letters, not Greek, from the time of Constantine, already a Christian, and of almost all the emperors after him: CONCORDIA ORBIS, with this legend normally placed below a representation of the cross.[36] An innumerable number of coins of the popes would be found if you had ever ruled in Rome. No such coins are found, either in gold or silver, and they are not mentioned as seen by anyone, and yet it was necessary at that time for anyone who held power at Rome to have his own coinage—even with a depiction of the Savior and Peter. Alas for the ignorance of mankind! You do not perceive that, if the Donation of Constantine is true, the emperor—I am speaking of the one in the Latin West—has nothing left. What sort of Roman emperor or king will he be, if any holder of his

kingdom who lacks another kingdom has absolutely nothing at all? But if therefore it is plain that Sylvester did not have possession, in other words that Constantine did not hand over possession, there will be no doubt that, as I have said, he did not even give the right to possess, unless you assert that the right was given but that for some reason possession was not assigned. Thus did he clearly give what he realized would not at all come into being? Did he give what he could not assign? Did he give what could not pass into the hands of the recipient before it ceased to exist? Did he give a gift that would be not be valid until five hundred years later or never? To talk or think like this is lunacy.

: III :

But now it is time, lest I go on too long, to administer a mortal blow to my opponents' case, already battered and mangled, and to slice its throat with a single stroke. Virtually all history that is worthy of the name reports that Constantine was a Christian from childhood together with his father Constantius even well before the papacy of Sylvester. So Eusebius, author of an ecclesiastical history which Rufinus, a man of considerable erudition, translated into Latin, adding two books devoted to his own time. Both of these men were near contemporaries of Constantine. Add to this the testimony of a Roman pontiff who did not merely participate in the course of these events but was in charge of them, not as a passive witness but as an active instigator, a narrator not of someone else's affairs but of his own. He is Pope Melchiades, who immediately preceded Sylvester, and this is what he says: *The Church has reached the point when not only peoples but even Roman emperors, who held sway over the whole world, might join together in the faith of Christ and its sacraments. Of these emperors, Constantine, a highly religious man, first openly espoused faith in the truth and made it*

34

27

permissible for those who lived anywhere in the world under his rule not only to become Christians but to build churches, and he arranged for the assignment of properties. Finally the aforementioned emperor provided immense largesse and started the construction of the first basilica of the see of St. Peter, so that he gave up his own imperial residence and granted it to St. Peter and his successors for their future use.[37] You see that Melchiades says Constantine gave nothing except the Lateran palace and the properties that Gregory very often mentions in his register. Where are those who do not allow us to question the validity of the Donation of Constantine, when the actual donation took place before Sylvester and consisted solely of private properties?

: IV :

35   Although this issue is clear and obvious, we must nevertheless discuss the document itself, which those blockheads keep putting forward. First of all, not only must we charge with dishonesty the person who wanted to pose as Gratian by making additions to Gratian's work, but we must also charge with ignorance those who think that the text of the document was included in Gratian's collection, since no scholars ever thought it was and it is missing in all the oldest editions of the decrees.[38] If Gratian had mentioned this matter anywhere, he would not have mentioned it where those persons put it, by interrupting the sequence of thought, but rather in the context of the settlement with Louis. Besides there are two thousand passages in the decrees which are at variance with the assertion of this text. One of these is where, as I have indicated above, the words of Melchiades occur. Some say that the person who added this chapter was called Palea,[39] either because that was really his name or because what he added on his own was, in comparison with Gratian, like chaff (*palea*) alongside wheat. Whatever the case may be, it is highly demeaning to suggest that the com-

piler of decrees either did not know what this man added or valued it highly and considered it authentic.

Fine, enough! We have won our case: first because Gratian does 36 not say what they mendaciously claimed, but rather — as can be grasped from innumerable passages — denies and refutes it, and second because they adduce an unknown person of no authority or consequence, who was so stupid that he added to Gratian material that could not be reconciled with all the rest of his utterances. Are you therefore advancing this person as the author? Do you rely upon the testimony of this one man, do you invoke his statement in confirmation of such an important matter against all kinds of proof? I should have expected you to show gold seals, marble inscriptions, a thousand authors. "But," you say, "Palea himself produces his author, displays the source of his history, and cites the testimony of Pope Gelasius together with many bishops: *It comes from the Acts of Sylvester*, he asserts, *which the blessed Pope Gelasius, in the Council of Seventy Bishops, mentions are read by Catholics, and he says that many churches imitate this in accordance with ancient custom — Acts in which Constantine is said etc.*" [40] Much earlier, in a discussion of which books should be read and which not, he had also said, *We know that the Acts of the blessed Sylvester, the high priest, are read by many Catholics from Rome, even though we have no idea of the name of the person who wrote them, and that churches imitate this example in accordance with ancient custom.*[41]

What wonderful authority this is, what wonderful testimony, 37 an unassailable demonstration! I grant you that Gelasius said this when he was speaking in the Council of Seventy Bishops. But he did not say, did he, that the item about the donation is read in the Acts of the most blessed Sylvester? He only says that the Acts of Sylvester are read, and at Rome, and that many other churches follow the authority of Rome's church. This I do not deny. I concede it, I admit it, I present myself as a witness along with

Gelasius. But what does it do for you, except that you appear to have deliberately lied in producing witnesses? No one knows the name of the man who wrote this in the decrees, and he is the only one who says it. No one knows the name of the man who wrote the history, and he is the only one brought forward as a witness, and falsely too. Do you, good and sagacious people, think that this is sufficient and more than sufficient as evidence for something so important? Look at how great a difference there is between my judgment and yours: Not even if the donation were contained in the Acts of Sylvester would I think it should be reckoned authentic, since that history is not history but a poetic and very brazen fabrication — as I will show later — and no one else of the slightest authority makes mention of this donation. Even Jacopo da Voragine, as an archbishop enthusiastically inclined towards the clergy, nevertheless in his Acts of the Saints kept silent about the Donation of Constantine as fictitious and unworthy of inclusion among the Acts of Sylvester.[42] In a way this was a judgment against those who might have written about the matter.

38   But this forger, this truly "straw man," the wheatless Palea, I want to grab by the neck and drag into court. What do you say, forger? How does it happen that we do not find this grant in the Acts of Sylvester? To be sure, this book is a rarity, hard to find and not in general circulation, but it is kept as the Fasti were formerly kept by the ancient Pontifices or the Sibylline Books by the Decemviri. It was written in the Greek language or in Syriac or in Chaldaean. Gelasius testifies that it was read by many Catholics, and Voragine mentions it. We too have seen thousands of copies written long ago, and they are read out in almost every cathedral on Sylvester's birthday. Yet no one says that he has read there what you put in. No one says he has heard of it, or dreamt of it. Or perhaps there is some other history. And what will that be? I know of no other, and I cannot make out that any other is meant by you, since you talk about the one that Gelasius reports as being

read in many churches. Yet in this history we have not found that grant of yours. But if it is not in the text of the life of Sylvester, why have you claimed that it is? Why in a matter of such importance have you dared to jest and to play off the desire of simple folk?

But I am foolish to attack that man's brazenness rather than the madness of those who have believed him. If anyone among the Greeks, Hebrews, or barbarians were to say that this was transmitted to memory, would you not ask for the author to be named, the book to be produced, and the passage to be expounded by a trustworthy critic before you believed him? Now your own language and a very famous book are at issue, and either you make no inquiry about such an unbelievable item or, when you fail to discover the written text, you show such headlong credulity that you accept it as written and as true. Fortified by this ascription, you confound earth and sea, and, as if there were no doubt at all, you pursue those who do not believe you with the terrifying prospect of war and other threats. Good Lord, what strength, what divinity there is in the truth, which, on its own, defends itself without great effort from all treachery and deceit. Thus not undeservedly, when a dispute arose at the court of King Darius as to what was strongest of all, and one person gave one opinion and another another, the palm was awarded to truth. Since my argument is with priests and not with laymen, ecclesiastical examples, rather than secular ones, ought to be produced. When Judas Maccabaeus sent his envoys to Rome to gain a treaty and friendship from the Senate, he made sure that the words of the treaty were incised on bronze and carried to Jerusalem.[43] I say nothing about the stone tablets of the Decalogue, which God gave to Moses. But this donation of Constantine, so splendid and so unexampled, can be proven by no document at all, whether on gold or on silver or on bronze or on marble or, finally, in books, but only, if we believe that man, on paper or parchment. Since the opinion was handed

39

down from generation to generation that human achievements were to be destroyed at one time by water and at another by fire, Jobal, the inventor of music (according to Josephus),[44] inscribed his teaching on two columns — one in brick against fire, the other in stone against water, both of which lasted, by his own account, to Josephus' own time — in order that his benefaction to mankind should exist forever. Even among the Romans when they were rustic and uncultivated, when there was slight and scarce literacy, the laws of the Twelve Tables were nonetheless incised on bronze. After the city was captured and burnt by the Gauls they were subsequently discovered intact. To such an extent does prudent foresight overcome the two greatest forces in human affairs, the length of time and the violence of fortune. Did Constantine really sign a donation of the world only on papyrus and with ink? The man who concocted this story, whoever he was, went out of his way to claim that Constantine said that he thought there would be no shortage of people to rescind this donation out of godless greed. Are you afraid of this, Constantine, and are you not exercising caution to stop those who would take Rome away from Sylvester from making off with the charter too? Tell me, is Sylvester himself doing nothing on his own behalf? Is he turning over everything to Constantine? Is he so indifferent and slothful in a matter of such importance? Does he take no thought for himself, no thought for the Church, no thought for posterity? Look at the man to whom you would entrust the administration of the Roman empire! He who falls asleep in a matter of such great consequence and of such potential profit or danger will be quite unable, once the grant charter has disappeared, to give proof of the donation after so much time has passed.

40   The madman calls it the *text of the grant*. Do you — I prefer to attack him as if he were present before me — do you speak of a donation of the world as a grant? Do you claim that this is written in

the *text* and that Constantine used that kind of language? If the title is absurd, what should we think of the rest of it?

> *Emperor Constantine, on the fourth day after his baptism, conveyed*   41
> *to the pontiff of the Church of Rome a grant, so that throughout the*
> *entire Roman world priests should consider him their head, just as*
> *judges their king.*[45]

This is contained in the actual history of Sylvester, which leaves no doubt where the word grant was indicated. But, just like those who concoct lies, he begins from the truth in order to win trust for the falsehoods that follow, just as Sinon in Virgil: *I shall tell you everything that happened, king, truthfully, he said, and I shall not deny that I am of the people of Argos.*[46] This comes first. After that he puts in the lies. This is what our Sinon does here, when he adds, after starting with the truth:

> *Among other things the following is said in this grant: We have*   42
> *judged it useful, together with all our satraps and the entire Senate,*
> *and the Optimates too, along with all people subject to the rule of the*
> *Church of Rome, that, just as the blessed Peter is seen to have been*
> *established as the vicar of God on earth, so too do the pontiffs in*
> *place of the prince of the apostles obtain from us and our empire the*
> *concession of a princely power of greater extent than the clemency of*
> *our earthly imperial serenity appeared to possess.*

You scoundrel, you miscreant, the same history that you cite in your support reports that for a long time no one in the senatorial order wanted to accept the Christian religion and that Constantine bribed the poor to undergo baptism: and you say that straightaway within the first days the Senate, the Optimates, the satraps, as if they were already Christians, issued a decree with the emperor about adorning the Church of Rome. Why do you want to bring in *satraps?*[47] You blockhead, you dolt! Do emperors talk

that way? Are Roman decrees normally drafted like that? Who ever heard of satraps being named in the deliberations of the Romans? I cannot recall reading that anyone, either in Rome or even in the provinces of the Romans, was ever named a satrap. But this person speaks of the emperor's satraps and puts them in charge of the Senate, even though all honors, even those conferred upon the prince himself, are only decreed by the Senate or by the Senate jointly with the Roman people. Hence we see written on old stones, bronze tablets, or coins the two letters SC, i.e. *senatus consulto* (by decree of the Senate), or the four letters SPQR, meaning *Senatus Populusque Romanus* (the Senate and Roman People). And, as Tertullian recounts,[48] when Pontius Pilate wrote about the marvelous works of Christ to Tiberius Caesar, not to the Senate — magistrates had normally written to the Senate about great events —, the Senate took this as a slight and rebuffed Tiberius' proposal to have Jesus worshipped as a god, by showing only silent indignation over the offense to senatorial dignity, while ensuring that he was not worshipped as a god, so that you might know the strength of senatorial authority. Why do you talk about Optimates? We assume that these are either the leading men in the state — why should they be named, when other magistrates are passed over in silence? — or that they are not the Populares, who curry the goodwill of the People, but rather partisans and defenders of every noble citizen and of good parties, as Cicero put it in one of his speeches.[49] Thus we say that Julius Caesar was a Popularis before the destruction of the Republic, and Cato belonged to the Optimates. Sallust has explained the difference between the two.[50] Neither are these Optimates reported to have been involved in consultation any more than the Populares or all other worthy people. No surprise if the Optimates are involved when *all people*, if we trust the man, deliberated with the Senate and the emperor, and, for that matter, people *subject to the Church of Rome!* What people is this? The Roman people? Why not say

"Roman people" rather than "subject people"? What is this new insult to the Quirites, whom the best of poets eulogized: *You, Roman, take care to rule over peoples with your imperial power.*[51] So the people that rules over other peoples is itself called a subject people. This is unheard of. For, as Gregory attests in many of his letters,[52] the Roman emperor differs from all other rulers in this particular point: he alone is the leader of a free people. But even if what you claim be granted, are not other peoples also subject? Or do you also have other people in mind? How could it happen in three days that all peoples subject to the rule of the Church of Rome were on hand for that decree? The dregs of the people did not give their opinion, did they? Tell me, would Constantine call a people subject before he had subjected them to the Roman pontiff? How is it that those who are called subject are said to have participated in passing the decree? How is it they are said to have decreed precisely that they be subject and that the person to whom they were already subject should have them as his subjects? What else are you doing, miserable man, except to show that you have the will to deceive, but not the ability?

> *Choosing the very prince of the apostles, or his vicars, to be strong*   43
> *advocates for us with God. And like our terrestrial imperial power,*
> *we have decreed honor with veneration for his sacrosanct Roman*
> *church, and that the most sacred seat of the blessed Peter be gloriously*
> *exalted more than our empire and earthly throne, in that we assign*
> *to him power, glory, dignity, and the vigor and distinction of empire.*

Come back to life, Lactantius,[53] just for a moment, and shut up the gross and monstrous braying of this ass. He is so enchanted by the sound of turgid vocabulary that he repeats the same things and regurgitates what he has already said. Did imperial scribes in your time talk like that, or even imperial lackeys? Constantine chose those people not as advocates, but *to be advocates.* He inserted that *to be* to make a more harmonious prose rhythm. A fine

reason to speak like a barbarian, to make your utterance go more prettily, as if anything pretty could be found in such coarseness. *Choosing the very prince of the apostles, or his vicars:* you do not choose Peter, do you, at the same time as the vicars who succeeded him? Either you choose him with the others excluded or them with him excluded. He calls the Roman pontiffs *vicars of Peter,* as if Peter is still alive or all the others are of lesser eminence than Peter was. Is it not also barbarous to talk about *us and our empire?* As if the empire had a mind and an authority to grant anything. Nor was he content to say *obtain* without also saying *granted,* when one or the other would have sufficed. That *strong advocates* is very elegant. Of course he wants them strong, so they will not be corrupted by bribes or slip back from fear. And that *terrestrial imperial power* is two adjectives without a conjunction. That *honor with veneration,* that *clemency of our imperial serenity!* It reeks of Lactantian eloquence when the power of empire is addressed, to speak of *serenity* and *clemency* instead of *amplitude* and *majesty.* How inflated with swollen pride, as in that *gloriously exalted* through *glory, power, dignity, vigor and distinction of empire,* which seems taken over from the Book of Revelation, where it is said: *Worthy is the lamb that was slain to receive courage, divinity, wisdom, strength, honor, and blessing.*[54] Frequently, as will emerge later, Constantine is made to take over epithets of God and to affect an imitation of the language of Sacred Scripture, which he had never read.

44   *And we sanction by decree that he have primacy over the four sees of Alexandria, Antioch, Jerusalem, and Constantinople, as well as over all churches of God in the whole globe of earth. Furthermore, the pontiff who in the course of time has stood over the sacrosanct Roman church shall exist as loftier and leader[55] to all the priests of the entire world, and whatever pertains to the worship of God and to guaranteeing the faith of Christians or their stability shall be arranged according to his judgment.*

Here I pass over the linguistic barbarisms, such as *leader to the priests* instead of *leader of the priests*, and the fact that he uses in the same context *stand over* and *exist*, and that when he said *in the whole globe of earth* he added *of the entire world*, as if he wants to include something different or the heavens, which are part of the world, although a good part of the globe of the earth was not under Rome. He also distinguished the *faith of the Christians or their stability*, as if they could not coexist. He mixed together decree and sanction and, as if Constantine had not made his decision earlier with all the others, makes him issue a decree and then sanction it like a punishment, and, for that matter, sanction it together with the people. What Christian would be able to put up with this and not chastise, rigorously and severely, the pope who puts up with this and gladly hears and proclaims it: although the Roman see received its primacy from Christ, and the Eighth Synod declared it, according to Gratian and many of the Greeks, it is said to have received this from Constantine, who was barely a Christian, as if from Christ. Would that very modest emperor have been willing to say this, and that very pious pontiff to hear it? Away with such serious wrongdoing on the part of either of them!

What of something much more absurd: would the nature of things allow someone to talk about Constantinople as one of the patriarchal sees, when it was then neither patriarchal nor a see, nor a Christian city, nor was it so called, nor was it yet founded, nor was the foundation envisioned? The grant was made three days after Constantine became a Christian, when the city was still Byzantium, not Constantinople. I am a liar myself if this idiot does not also admit this, for he writes near the end of the grant:

> *Wherefore we have considered it appropriate for our empire and our power to be transferred for the eastern territories and for a state to be built named for us in the best place of the province Byzantia, and for our empire to be established there.*

45

If he wanted to transfer the empire somewhere else, he had not yet done it; if he wanted to establish his imperial rule there, he had not yet done it; thus, if he had any intention of building a city, he had not yet built it. He would therefore not have made mention of patriarchal status, of one of four sees, of a Christian city, named for himself and already founded. According to the story that Palea invokes as evidence, he had not even thought of founding a city. This creature, whether he is Palea or someone else whom Palea is following, fails to see that he is in disagreement with this story, whereby Constantine is said to have issued a decree, not by his own volition but in a dream sent by God, not at Rome but at Byzantium, not within a few days but a good many years later, concerning founding a city and giving his name to it as he has been commanded when asleep. Who does not see that whoever composed the text of this grant lived long after the time of Constantine? When he wanted to embellish his falsehood, what he had said before escaped him — that these events took place at Rome on the third day after the emperor was baptized. So the hoary old proverb applies very properly to him: *Liars should have good memories.*[56]

46   What about his reference to the *province Byzantia?* There was a town Byzantium, a place in no way big enough for so great a city. For Constantinopolis incorporated old Byzantium in its walls, whereas this man says that the city was to be founded in the *best place* in it. Does he want Thrace, where Byzantium had been placed, to be in the east, when it lies to the north? Constantine had, I suppose, no idea of the place that he had chosen for founding a city — under what sky it lay, whether it was a city or a province, what its size was.

47   *To the churches of the blessed apostles Peter and Paul we have granted properties of our possessions to guarantee the lights, and we*

have enriched those churches with various items, and by our sacred imperial ordinance we have turned over to them through our largesse, no less in the east than in the west and even in the northern and southern sectors, that is — in Judaea, Greece, Asia, Thrace, Africa, and Italy as well as various islands, on this express condition that everything be in the hands of our most blessed father Sylvester, the supreme pontiff, and his successors.

You miserable dog, did Rome have churches, or rather temples, dedicated to Peter and Paul? Who built them? Who would have dared to build them? After all, as history tells us, nowhere was there any place for Christians apart from secret places and hidden dens. If there had been any temples at Rome dedicated to those apostles, they would not have required great lamps to be lit inside them. They were little shrines, not buildings; chapels, not temples; places of prayer in private dwellings, not public places of worship. No one therefore had to worry about temple lamps before there were the temples themselves. What are you talking about when you make Constantine speak of Peter and Paul as *blessed,* but Sylvester, when he is still alive, as *most blessed,* and his own ordinance as *sacred* when he had been a pagan shortly before? Does so much have to be provided for keeping up the lamps that the whole world is worn down? Anyhow, what are these properties, particularly landed ones? We normally say, "our possessions of property," not *property of our possessions.* You give properties, and you do not reveal what properties. You have enriched *with various items,* and you do not indicate when or with what. You want *sectors* of the world to be in the hands of Sylvester, and you do not explain how they are to be handled. You made those grants earlier. Why do you specify that you have begun today to honor the Roman church and to make the grant to it? You make the grant today, you make the enrichment today: Why do you say *We have granted* and *We*

have enriched? What are you talking about or what are you thinking, you beast? My argument is with the man who invented this
fiction, not with the outstanding emperor Constantine.

48   But why do I look for any discretion or any learning in you,
who are endowed with no talent and no literary taste? You say
lights when you mean *lamps,* and *transferred for the eastern territories*
when you mean *transferred to the eastern territories.* Besides, what are
those four sectors? What do you consider eastern? Thrace? As I
have already said, it lies to the north. Judaea? It lies more to the
south, inasmuch as it is near Egypt. Again, what is western? Italy?
But these events were taking place in Italy, which no one living
there calls western, although we say that the Spains are in the
west. Italy extends in one direction to the south, in the other to
the north, rather than to the west. What is northern? Thrace? But
you want Thrace to be in the east. Asia? This alone includes the
whole east, but it has the north in common with Europe. What is
southern? Africa definitely? But why do you not propose some
province by name, unless by chance the Ethiopians were under
Roman rule. Anyhow, Asia and Africa do not belong when we divide the world into four parts and mention by name the regions of
individual ones, but only when we divide into three: Asia, Africa,
Europe. Unless you mean Asia for the province of Asia, and Africa for that province which is near the Gaetulians, I do not see
why they should be singled out. Would Constantine have spoken
this way, when he was conjuring up the four sectors of the world,
so as to name these regions and not to name all the rest? Would
he begin with Judaea, which is counted a part of Syria and no
longer Judaea, with Jerusalem destroyed, with the Jews driven out
and nearly annihilated, to such an extent that I think scarcely anyone stayed in his own country but took up residence in other nations? Where then *was* Judaea? It was no longer called Judaea,
since we see today that its name has been wiped off the earth. Just
as Canaan ceased to be called Canaan after the Canaanites were

wiped out and the name was changed to Judaea by the new inhabitants, so too did Judaea cease to be called by that name when foreign peoples moved into it. You specify *Judaea, Thrace, islands*, but you do not think that the Spains, the Gauls, and the Germans need to be named. Although you speak about other language groups — Hebrew, Greek, barbarian, you say nothing about any of the provinces where Latin is spoken. All right, I see that you have omitted them in order to include them later in your donation. But were so many provinces in the west insufficient to cover the expense of maintaining lamps without help from the rest of the world? I pass over your statement that these grants were made through your *largesse*, not therefore, as others claim, because you were cured of leprosy. Besides, anyone who makes a payment in place of a gift would be a boor.

To the blessed Sylvester, his [Peter's] vicar, as of now we hand over   49
the Lateran palace of our empire, then the diadem — that is, the
crown on our head and at the same time the Phrygian tiara and the
superhumeral band (which is the strap that normally goes around the
imperial neck), but also the purple cloak and the scarlet tunic and all
imperial vestments, or the rank of commanders of the imperial cavalry. We confer on him as well the imperial sceptres and at the same
time all standards and banners and various imperial decorations,
and every procession of our imperial eminence and the glory of our
power. And for men of a different rank, the very reverend clergy
serving the holy Roman church, we sanction that pinnacle of exceptional authority and prominence with whose glory our most illustrious Senate seems to be adorned, namely to be made patricians and
consuls, and we have promulgated that they be decorated in all other
imperial dignities. Just as the imperial militia exists as decorated, so
have we decreed that the clergy of the holy Roman church be
adorned. Just as the imperial authority is organized by different
offices — chamberlains indeed, door-keepers, and all bed-mates, so do

we wish the holy Roman church to be decorated. In order that the pontifical splendor may gleam most brilliantly, we also decree that the clergy of the same holy Roman church be mounted on mounts decorated with napkins and linens that are of the whitest color, and that they be distinguished in the same way as our Senate, which makes use of shoes with felt socks — that is, with white linen. Thus will the celestial ranks be adorned like the terrestrial, to the glory of God.

O holy Jesus, will you not respond from the whirlwind to this man who is rolling out sentences without any command of his language? Will you not thunder? Will you not cast avenging bolts of lightning against such blasphemy? Do you put up with such disgrace in your own house? Can you hear this, can you see this, and yet ignore it for so long by closing your eyes? But *you are longsuffering and full of pity.*[57] Yet I fear that this longsufferingness of yours may be rather rage and condemnation, such as it was against those of whom you said: *I gave them up according to the lust of their heart; they will go in their own devisings,*[58] and elsewhere: *I have handed them over to their wicked mind, so that they may do what they ought not to do, because they have not shown that they have knowledge of me.*[59] Order me, Lord, I beg you, to shout against them, and they may by chance be converted. You Roman pontiffs, the model of all criminality for other pontiffs, you disgraceful *scribes and Pharisees who sit in the seat of Moses*[60] and do the deeds of Dathan and Abiron,[61] will the vestments, the appurtenances, the pomp, the horses, in short the lifestyle of an emperor thus befit the vicar of Christ? What does a priest have to do with an emperor? Did Sylvester put on those vestments? Did he move about with those appurtenances? Did he live and rule with all those servants in his house? The wickedest of men fail to understand that Sylvester ought rather to have put on the garments of Aaron, who was God's highest priest, than the vestments of a pagan ruler. But these matters will have to be addressed more thoroughly elsewhere. For the present, how-

ever, let us talk with this sycophant about his barbarous language. His idiotic diction exposes, all by itself, his utterly shameless lie.

We hand over, he says, *the Lateran palace of our empire*: as if he had 50 wrongly put the gift of the palace among the decorations, he repeated it again when dealing with donations. *Then the diadem*: as if those present do not understand, he glosses, *that is, the crown*. But here he did not add *of gold*, although later, treating the same subject, he says, *of purest gold and precious gems*. This ignorant man was unaware that a diadem was made of cloth, or perhaps of silk. Hence the wise and often told story of the king, *who is said, before putting on his head the diadem that had been given to him, to have held and long pondered it, and declared, "O cloth, more noble than fortunate! If anyone really knew with how much anxiety, danger, and misery you are fraught, he would not want to pick you up even if you were lying on the ground.*[62] This forger of ours cannot conceive that what kings now normally supplement with a gold band and gems was made of anything other than gold. But Constantine was not a king, nor would have made bold to call himself a king or to adorn himself with kingly ceremonial: he was Commander of the Romans, not king. Wherever there is a king, there is no republic, but in a republic there have been many called Commander, even at the same time. For Cicero frequently writes thus: *M. Cicero Commander sends greetings to the Commander*, whoever he may be. Of course afterwards the Roman emperor is distinctively called Commander as the Commander-in-Chief.

And at the same time the Phrygian tiara and the superhumeral band 51 *(which is the strap that normally goes around the imperial neck)*: Who ever heard of a *Phrygian tiara* in Latin? Although you talk like a barbarian, you apparently want me to think this is the language of Constantine or Lactantius. In his play *Menaechmi* Plautus used the word *phrygio* for a clothesmaker, and Pliny calls embroidered garments *phrygions* because the Phrygians invented them.[63] But what would a *Phrygian tiara* signify? You fail to explain what is unclear,

and you explain what is altogether clear. You say that the superhumeral band is a strap and yet you do not know what a strap is. For you do not imagine that a leather band, which is what we mean by a strap, was put around the emperor's neck as an ornament. We call reins and whips straps because they are made of leather. But if mention be made of golden straps, it can only be understood as referring to gilded reins that are put around the neck of a horse or some other animal. In my opinion this point has escaped you, and when you propose to put a strap on the emperor's neck or Sylvester's you are making a man, a ruler, and a supreme pontiff into a horse or an ass.

52   *But also the purple cloak and the scarlet tunic:* Since Matthew speaks of a *scarlet cloak* and John of a *purple garment,*[64] this forger wanted to combine both of them together in the same place. But if the color is the same, as the Evangelists indicate, why were you not satisfied with one name, just as they were? Unless you understand by *purple,* in the way that ignorant people talk today, a kind of silk fabric of white color. The fact is that purple is a fish in whose blood wool is dyed,[65] and therefore the name has been applied to the cloth from the dye. Its color can be taken as red, although it may be on the black side and very close to the color of dried blood—almost violet. Hence blood is called purple by Homer and Virgil,[66] and so is porphyry, whose color is very like amethyst. The Greeks actually call purple "porphyry." Perhaps you are not unaware that scarlet can be taken to mean "red," but why would he put *scarlet* when we would say *crimson?* And I would swear that you simply do not know what kind of a garment the *cloak* is. And, lest he betray himself as a liar by going into more detail about individual garments, he summed them all up in a single phrase, *all imperial vestments.* Look here, everything the emperor is given to wearing in war, in hunting, in banquets, and in games? What is more idiotic than to say that all the emperor's vestments are appropriate for a pontiff? But how delicately he adds *or the rank of commanders*

of the imperial cavalry! He says *or*: he wanted to distinguish these two in turn, as if they had much similarity between them, and he slides from imperial dress to equestrian rank with no sense at all. He wants to utter something marvelous, but he is afraid of being caught lying and therefore, with inflated cheeks and swollen throat, *he makes a mindless noise.*[67]

We confer on him as well the imperial sceptres: What a way to talk! 53 What glamor! What balance! What are those *imperial sceptres*? There is just one sceptre, not several. If only the emperor carried a sceptre, will the pontiff carry a sceptre in his hand? Why shall we not give him a sword, a helmet, and a javelin? *And at the same time all standards and banners*: What do you understand by *standards*? Standards are either statues — we often say "standards and panels" for "sculptures and pictures" since the ancients did not paint on walls but panels — or else legionary ensigns, hence *standards and matched eagles.*[68] From the former meaning little statues and sculptures are called standing knick-knacks. Was Constantine giving Sylvester his statues or his military eagles? What could be more absurd? But what *banners* is supposed to mean I have no idea. May God destroy you, wickedest of mortals, for ascribing barbarous speech to an age of learning. *And various imperial decorations*: Because he said banners, he thought he had been clear enough and therefore lumped all the rest in a general phrase. And how often he belabors *imperial*: as if certain decorations are more appropriate to a commander-in-chief than to a consul, a dictator, or a Caesar. *And every procession of our imperial eminence and glory of our power*: "He throws out bombast and polysyllabic words," [69] — Darius, *King of Kings and of the race of gods*,[70] never speaking except in the plural. What is that *imperial procession*? Is it not that of a "cucumber that is curled up in the grass and grows into a belly?"[71] Do you think that Caesar held a triumph whenever he stepped outside his house, as the Pope now does, preceded by white horses that his servants lead saddled and adorned? Not to mention other absurdi-

ties, there is nothing emptier, nothing more inappropriate for a Roman pontiff than this. Also, what is this *glory*? Would a Latin-speaker call glory, as is the custom in the Hebrew language, the pomp and the splendor of pageantry? Instead of "soldiers" would he say *militia*, which we have borrowed from the Hebrews, whose books Constantine or his scribes had never looked upon.

54 But how great is your generosity, Emperor, who are not content to have adorned the pontiff without adorning the entire clergy as well. You say that *being made patricians and consuls* is the *pinnacle of exceptional authority and prominence*. Who ever heard of senators or other men being "made" patricians? Consuls are made, not patricians, who come either from a patrician house—which is also called senatorial, inasmuch as senators are *conscript fathers*—or from an equestrian house or plebeian one. It is more important to be a senator than a patrician, since a senator is one of the chosen advisors of the republic, whereas a patrician is just someone who traces his origin from a senatorial house. That means that a senator or one of the *conscript fathers* is not straightaway also a patrician. My Roman friends nowadays behave ridiculously when they call their governor a senator, since a senate cannot consist of one man, and a senator must necessarily have colleagues. The man who is now called a senator performs the office of governor. "But the patrician rank is found in many books," you say. I know, but in those that talk about the post-Constantinian period. Therefore the grant was made after Constantine. But can clerics be made consuls too? Latin clerics deny themselves marriage. Will they become consuls? Will they levy soldiers and go out with legions and auxiliary troops into provinces they have been allotted? Will servants and slaves become consuls, not just two of them, as used to be the case, but hundreds and thousands? Will servants in the employ of the Roman church be assigned the rank of general? I was foolish enough to marvel that the Pope was said to have that rank! Servants will be generals, clerics soldiers: Will soldiers become

clerics or wear military decorations? Unless you are bestowing the decorations of a general on clerics as a whole — well, in that case I do not know what you are talking about. Who fails to see that this fiction was concocted by persons who wanted complete license for themselves to dress up? I would imagine that if somewhere various games took place among the demons who live in the air, those creatures would be engaged in copying the ritual of clerics, their pageantry, and their luxury, and they would derive their greatest pleasure from this kind of theatrical competition.

Should I attack the foolishness of ideas more than words? You 55
have heard about the ideas. Here is the foolishness of words: that he claims the Senate *should be adorned*, as if it were not already adorned, and, for that matter, *adorned with glory*. And he wants to turn what is happening into something that has already happened, as with *we have promulgated* instead of "we are promulgating," since the language sounds more resonant that way. He states the same thing in the present and past tenses, as *we decree* and *we have decreed*. Everything is stuffed with these words — *we decree, we adorn, imperial, imperatorial, power, glory*; and he has put *exists* in place of *is*, since existing implies prominence or superiority, and *indeed* for "of course" and *bed-mates* for "companions." Bed-mates are those who sleep together and have intercourse, and must naturally be understood to be whores. He adds those with whom he sleeps, lest, I suppose, he be frightened by nocturnal apparitions: he adds *chamberlains*, he adds *door-keepers*. It is not irrelevant why these details are mentioned by him: he is instructing a ward or an adolescent son, not an old man. Like a doting father, he prepares for the boy everything of which his tender years have need, as David did for Solomon.

For the fiction to be fleshed out in every particular, *horses* are 56
provided for the clergy, to keep them from sitting on donkeys in the way that Christ sat on an ass, and they are not "covered" or "saddled with coverings of white color," but *decorated with white*

color. But with what coverings? Not with cloths, Babylonian or of any other kind, but *with napkins and linens.* Napkins go with the dining table, linens with beds. And as if there were any doubt as to what their color is, he glosses *that is, of the whitest color.* A style worthy of Constantine, an eloquence worthy of Lactantius, not only in other places but also in that phrase *be mounted on mounts!* Although he said nothing about senatorial garb—nothing about the broad stripe, the purple, or anything else, he thought he ought to speak about the *shoes.* He did not call them "lunettes" but *felt socks,* or rather *with felt socks,* which, in the way of this hopeless man, he explains *that is, with white linen,* as if felt socks are linen. At the moment I cannot think of anywhere that I have found felt socks apart from Martial, whose epigram inscribed *Hairy Felt Socks* goes as follows: *Wool did not make these socks, but the beard of a smelly goat. / His foot could be hidden in the Bay of Kinyps.*[72] Therefore felt socks are not linen, and they are not white,—those objects with which our two-footed ass says not that the feet of senators are shod, but with which *senators are distinguished.* As for *thus will the celestial ranks be adorned like the terrestrial, to the glory of God:* what do you call celestial, what terrestrial? How are the celestial adorned? You may know what glory that may be for God, but I think, if I have any credibility, that nothing is more hateful to God and to other men than clerics' taking so much license in secular matters. But why do I attack one individual point after another? I should run out of time if I try to mention, to say nothing of discuss, all of them.

57   *Before all else, however, we assign to the blessed Sylvester and to his successors, according to our indiction, the right to name anyone he wishes to the clergy at his pleasure and by his own decision and to include that person in the pious ranks of the pious clergy, and that no one whatsoever should consider that he is acting arrogantly.*

Who is this Melchizedek, who blesses Abraham the patriarch? Did Constantine, hardly yet a Christian, assign the privilege of making priests to the man by whom he was baptized and whom he calls blessed, as if Sylvester would not, and could not, have done this before? And with what menace he forbade anyone from blocking this: *no one whatsoever should consider that he is acting arrogantly.* With what choice diction: *to include that person in the pious ranks of the pious, . . . to the clergy. . . . the clergy,* and *indiction,* and *at his pleasure.* And again he goes back to the diadem:

> And so we have also decreed the following, that he and his successors ought to use the diadem — that is, the crown — made of purest gold and of precious gems, which we have granted to him from our own head, and this in honor of blessed Peter.

Once again he glosses *diadem,* since he was talking with barbarians with a short memory, and he adds *of purest gold,* in case you think that by chance some bronze or dross was mixed in. When he said *gems,* he adds *precious* out of a similar fear that you might perhaps suspect something cheap. Yet there is a greater difference between one gem and another than between gold and gold. Although he ought to have said *studded with gems,* he said *of gems.* Who fails to see that this was taken from that passage, which the pagan emperor had not read: *You have placed upon his head a crown of precious stone.*[73] Did the emperor speak in this way, by boasting about wearing his crown — if only emperors were crowned — and by insulting himself as someone who was afraid that men would not think he wore a crown *of purest gold with precious gems* unless he told them so. Listen to the reason why he talks like that: *in honor of blessed Peter,* as if Christ were not the most important cornerstone on which the temple of the Church has been built, but Peter, as he claims again later. If he wanted to venerate Peter so much, why did he not dedicate the Church's temple at Rome to him instead of to

John the Baptist? Look here, does not that barbarous way of talking attest that this nonsense was not concocted in the age of Constantine, but later?

58   We decree that *they ought to use*, in place of what it is we decree, namely "that they use": Uncultivated people commonly talk and write this way, "ordered that you ought to come" instead of "ordered that you come." And *we have decreed* and *we have granted*: as if this were not happening at the time but had happened at some other time.

59   *But the blessed Pope himself did not suffer the use of that crown of gold on top of the priestly crown, which he wears to the glory of the most blessed Peter.*

How bizarre is your foolishness, Constantine! You were just saying that you were putting the crown on the Pope's head in honor of blessed Peter. Now you say that you are not doing that because Sylvester refuses it, and although you approve of his refusal, you nonetheless instruct him *to use a golden crown*, and what he thinks he should not do himself you say his successors should do. I pass over your calling a tonsure a *crown* and the Roman pontiff a Pope, even though that title had not yet begun to be exclusively his.[74]

60   *But we have placed with our own hands upon his most holy head a Phrygian tiara shining with the most radiant whiteness, as a symbol of our Lord's resurrection, and holding his horse's bridle out of reverence for the blessed Peter we have assumed for him the role of a squire, as we ordain that all his successors individually use the same tiara in processions in imitation of our imperial power.*

Does not this fiction-monger appear to be a fraud, not through inadvertence but deliberately and designedly, and on all sides to furnish grips with which to catch him? In the same passage he says both that the *Lord's resurrection* is symbolized by a Phrygian tiara and that it is an *imitation* of the emperor's *power*: these two things

are completely incompatible. With God as my witness, I cannot find the words, I cannot find the brutality of language for striking down this utterly shameless wretch. All the words he keeps spewing out are full of lunacy. He not only makes Constantine similar in office to Moses, who adorned the High Priest on the order of God, but he makes him an expounder of secret mysteries — something extremely difficult even for those who have long been immersed in sacred texts. Why did you not also make Constantine the chief pontiff, as indeed many emperors were, so that his decorations might be more conveniently transferred to another supreme pontiff? But you knew no history. And so I thank God for this too, that he allowed such an utterly unspeakable idea to occur only to the stupidest possible person. Further points show this as well, for he adduces Moses' *assuming the role of a squire* for Aaron, who was sitting on his horse, not in the middle of Israel but among the Canaanites and Egyptians, in other words in a pagan state where there was not so much an empire of the world as an empire of demons and of peoples worshipping demons.

> *Accordingly, to ensure that the pontifical preeminence not be demeaned but adorned with glory and power greater than the dignity of imperial rule, behold — we give over to the most blessed pontiff and universal Pope, Sylvester, not only our palace but the city of Rome and all the provinces, places, and cities of Italy or the western territories, and we have decreed that they be managed by him and his successors through our pragmatic sanction and that they remain under the law of the holy Roman church.* 61

We have already treated this at length in the speeches we assigned to the Romans and Sylvester. At this juncture it is pertinent to remark that no one would have acted to include all nations in a single phrase of donation, and that no one who had previously plodded through the most minute details such as *strap, shoes, and linen horsecloths* would not explicitly name provinces which today have

one or more kings of their own or rulers equal to kings. Obviously this forger had no idea which provinces were under Constantine and which were not, for certainly they were not all under him. When Alexander died, we observe that specific territories were divided up among his generals. The lands and rulers that were subject to the rule of Cyrus, either voluntarily or by force, were specified by Xenophon.[75] The names of Greek and barbarian kings, their race, country, character, strength, beauty, size of navy and the approximate size of their army were registered by Homer in a catalogue,[76] which not only many Greeks but also our own Latin writers — Ennius, Virgil, Lucan, Statius, and some others — have taken as a model. In the division of the Promised Land all the little villages were described by Joshua and Moses. And you balk at listing even provinces? You name only *western provinces:* What are the boundaries of the West? Where do they begin, where end? The limits of west, east, south, and north are not so certain and fixed as those of Asia, Africa, and Europe, are they? You leave out necessary words, you pile on superfluous ones. You say *provinces, places, and cities:* are not provinces and cities *places?* When you have said *provinces,* you add *cities,* as if these would not be understood as included. But it is not surprising that a man who relinquishes such a large part of the world should pass over the names of cities and provinces and, as if overcome with lethargy, be unaware of what he is saying. *Of Italy or the western territories:* as if he meant one or the other, when he meant both — speaking of *provinces of the territories,* although they are rather "territories of the provinces," and in saying *that they remain* instead of "that they will remain."

62   *Wherefore we have considered it appropriate for our empire and our power to be transferred for the eastern territories, and in the best place of the province Byzantia for a state to be built named for us and our empire to be established there.*

I say nothing of his talking about *building a state*, when a city, not a state, is meant. Similarly I pass over the *province Byzantia*. If you are really Constantine, give your reason for choosing that place above all others for founding a city. Moving yourself somewhere else after handing over Rome is not so much fitting as necessary, nor can you call yourself an emperor, who have lost Rome and deserved the worst of the Roman name, which you are tearing apart, nor can you call yourself king, as no one before you has done, unless you call yourself king because you have ceased to be a Roman. But you advance one reason that is certainly honest:

> *For where the prince of priests and the head of the Christian religion*   63
> *has been established by the heavenly ruler, it is not just for the earthly*
> *ruler to have power there.*

Foolish David, foolish Solomon, foolish Ezechiel and Josiah and all the other kings, foolish and insufficiently pious, who kept on living with the high priests in the city of Jerusalem and did not abandon the entire city to them! Constantine knows more in three days than they were able to know in a whole lifetime. And you speak of the *heavenly ruler* because he has accepted an earthly empire, unless you are referring to God—for your words are ambiguous—, by Whom you are mendaciously claiming that the earthly principality of the priests was established over the city of Rome and all the other places.

> *Furthermore, everything that we have established and confirmed*   64
> *through this sacred imperial charter and through other divine decrees*
> *we have decreed to remain untouched and unaltered down to the end*
> *of the world.*

Just now you had called yourself *earthly*, Constantine, now you call yourself *divine* and *sacred*. You lapse into paganism, and more than paganism: you make yourself a god, your words sacred, and your decrees immortal, for you order the world to keep your commands

untouched and unaltered. You do not consider who you are, only recently cleansed of the foulest slime of impiety and scarcely washed clean. Why did you not add: *not one jot or one tittle will pass* from this grant *until heaven and earth are no more?*[77] The kingdom of Saul, who was chosen by God, did not pass to his sons, the kingdom of David was divided under his grandson and subsequently wiped out: yet you decree by your own authority that the kingdom you have handed over without God will last until the end of the world. Who taught you that the world was going to perish so soon? I do not think that you have at this moment any trust in the poets who bear witness to this. Therefore you would not have said it, but someone else foisted it upon you. But the person who spoke so grandly and proudly starts to be afraid and to distrust himself, and so he launches entreaties:

> *Accordingly before the living God, who ordered us to reign, and before his terrible judgment seat we entreat all our successors, emperors and every nobleman, satraps too and the most resplendent Senate and the entire people in the entire world, and in time to come, to permit none of them in any way either to demolish this or for it to be torn asunder in any way.*

How just, how religious this adjuration! It is no different from a wolf, who entreats, on the basis of his innocence and good faith, all the other wolves and the shepherds, not to try to steal, in the case of the wolves, or recover, in the case of the shepherds, the sheep that he has carried off and divided among his sons and friends. What frightens you so, Constantine? If your work is not of God, it will be destroyed, but if it is of God, it will be incapable of being destroyed. But, I observe, you wanted to copy the Book of Revelation, where it is said: *For I testify to the one who hears all the words of the prophecy of this book—if anyone adds to these words, God will inflict upon him the torments described in this book, and if anyone subtracts from the words of this prophetic book, God will take away his part*

from the book of life and the holy city.[78] But you had never read the Book of Revelation. Therefore, those words are not yours.

> *If, moreover, anyone — which we do not believe — emerges as a falsifier in this context, let him be condemned and subjected to eternal damnation. Let him know that his enemies are the holy apostles of God, Peter and Paul, in the present and in the life to come, and let him be burned in the lower reaches of hell and waste away together with the devil and all who are wicked.*

65

Such terrorizing and such threatening are not characteristic of a secular ruler, but of old-school priests and keepers of the flame, and nowadays of ecclesiastics: so this is not the speech of Constantine, but of some dim-witted petty cleric, who has no idea of what he is saying or how he is saying it, someone who is fat and gross, belching out these phrases and these words while drunk and heated with wine. His words do not impinge upon anyone else but turn upon the author himself. First he says *subjected to eternal damnation*, then, as if more could be added, he wants to add something else and joins punishments *of the present life* after an eternity of punishments. When he terrifies us by the condemnation of God, he goes on to terrify us, as if it were something still greater, with the hatred of Peter, to whom he attaches Paul — I cannot imagine why, or why only Paul. With his typical sloth he goes back again to eternal punishments, as if he had not said this already. But if these threats and curses were really Constantine's, I would curse him in turn as a tyrant and destroyer of my nation, and I would threaten to take vengeance on him myself in my capacity as a Roman. Now, who would fear the curse of the greediest of men, mouthing words the way actors do and frightening others in the guise of Constantine? This is what it really means to be a hypocrite, if we take the Greek word literally — to hide your own identity under someone else's.[79]

66   *Reinforcing the page of this imperial decree by our very own hands,*
      we have placed it on the venerable body of the blessed Peter.

Was it paper or parchment, the page on which these things were
written down? In fact we call a page one or the other side of a so-
called leaf, just as a gathering has ten leaves but twenty pages.
What unheard-of and unbelievable nonsense! When I was a boy, I
remember asking someone who had written the Book of Job.
When he answered, "Job himself," I asked the further question of
how therefore he managed to mention his own death. This can be
said of many other books, although it is not appropriate to discuss
them here. For how can something that has not yet taken place be
accurately told? How can the tablets include something which he
admits himself occurred after the burial, so to speak, of the tablets? This is tantamount to saying that the page of the grant was
dead and buried before it was born, and yet never came back from
its death and burial, particularly since it was reinforced before it
was written—not merely with one of the emperor's hands but
with both. What is meant by *reinforcing* the page? With the emperor's signature or with his signet-ring? That would certainly be a
great reinforcement, much greater than if it had been entrusted to
bronze tablets. But there is no need of a bronze inscription, because the document is placed upon the body of the blessed Peter.
Why are you silent about Paul (lying together with Peter), when
both could provide more protection than if only the body of one
of them were there?

67   You see the cunning and malice of this most vicious Sinon. Because the Donation of Constantine cannot be exhibited, he has
therefore said that the grant is not on bronze tablets but on paper
sheets, and that it is hidden with the body of the most holy apostle, to keep us from boldly looking for it in the venerable tomb or,
if we were to do so, we would suppose that it had been ruined by
decay.

But where was the body of blessed Peter then? Certainly not in   68
the temple where it is now, not in a well protected and safe place.
Therefore the emperor would not have put his document there.
Did he forbear to entrust it to the very blessed Sylvester, as not
holy enough, not cautious enough, not diligent enough? O Peter
and Sylvester, holy pontiffs of the Roman church, to whom the
sheep of the Lord have been committed, why did you not protect
the document as committed to you? Why did you allow it to be
gnawed by worms, to rot with mould? Because, I suppose, your
bodies have also rotted away. Constantine acted stupidly. Once the
document has been reduced to dust, the legal force of the grant
has turned to dust at the same time.

And yet, as we see, a copy of the document is on show. What   69
rash person took it from the breast of the most holy apostle? No
one, I think, did this. So where does the copy come from? Doubtless one of the ancient writers ought to be adduced, and someone
no later than the time of Constantine. But no one is adduced. Perhaps a recent writer? Where did he get it? For anyone who has
put together a history of an earlier age either speaks at the dicta-
tion of the Holy Spirit or follows the authority of old writers and
naturally of those who wrote about their own time. Accordingly
whoever does not follow ancient writers will be one of those
whom the very antiquity of the events emboldens to lie. If that account is read at any point, it no more conforms with antiquity
than that foolish narration of Accursius, the writer of glosses, ac-
cords with Livy and other preeminent writers on Roman legates
who were dispatched to Greece to obtain laws.[80]

Given at Rome on the third day before the Kalends of April, when   70
Constantine Augustus was consul for the fourth time and Gallicanus
was consul for the fourth time.

He has specified the thirtieth of March so that we would think
this was done at the time of the holy days, which normally occur

at that time. And *when Constantine was consul for the fourth time and Gallicanus was consul for the fourth time:* amazing if both had been three times consul and turned out to be colleagues together in their fourth consulates, but even more amazing that the Augustus, who was a leper with elephantiasis, which as a disease stands out among others like an elephant among beasts, even wanted to take up the consulate, whereas king Azarias delegated his kingdom to his son Jotham and stayed in seclusion,[81] just as almost all lepers have done. By this single argument the entire grant is utterly refuted, destroyed, and overturned. And should anyone doubt whether he had to have been a leper before a consul, he should be aware both from medicine that this disease grows slowly over time and from knowledge of antiquity that a consulate begins in the month of January and is a year-long magistracy. Yet these events are assigned to the following March. Nor will I keep silent about the fact that *given* is normally written in personal correspondence, but not in other documents except among the uneducated. Letters are said to be given either "to someone" or "to someone's address" — to someone who carries the letters, such as a messenger, who would deliver and place them in the hand of the man to whom they are sent, or rather to someone's address for the letters to be delivered to the person to whom they are sent. But the grant that is allegedly Constantine's should not have been said to have been given, because it was not supposed to be delivered to anybody. Wherefore it should be apparent that the person who spoke this way was lying and had no idea how to invent what Constantine would plausibly have said or done.

71   Those who think that this person spoke the truth and defend him make themselves his allies, complicit in his foolishness and insanity. Yet they now have nothing with which they can decently excuse their opinion, not to say defend it. Is there anything decent about excusing an error when you refuse to accept a manifest truth just because some great men thought otherwise? They were great,

I say, in rank, not in wisdom or virtue. How can you tell whether those whom you follow would have persevered in their view, rather than abandoned it, if they had heard what you have heard? Furthermore it is highly inappropriate to want to give more credit to a man than to the truth — that is, to God. For some who have been overcome by all arguments are apt to answer me: "Why have so many supreme pontiffs believed that this was true?" You are my witnesses that you urge me where I would not go, and you force me unwillingly to speak ill of supreme pontiffs over whose mistakes I would rather draw a veil.

But let us continue to speak frankly — since this case cannot be 72 conducted in any other way — so that I may admit that they held that belief and did so without malice. Where is the surprise if they believe this, with the enticement of so much profit, when they believe many things, in their remarkable ignorance, without any visible prospect of profit? In the Ara Coeli do we not see, in that outstanding church and in an exceedingly venerable spot a painting of the story of the Sibyl and Octavian, allegedly on the authority of Innocent III who wrote the text? He also left an account of the destruction of the Temple of Peace on the day of the Savior's birth — at the time of the delivery of the Virgin.[82] These stories do more to overturn faith, because they are false, than to strengthen it, because they are miraculous. Does the vicar of truth dare to tell lies under the guise of piety and knowingly to implicate himself in this sin? Is he not telling lies? In fact he fails to see that, when he does this, he is disagreeing with the holiest of men. I leave others aside, but Jerome makes use of the testimony of Varro that there were ten Sibyls, and Varro composed his work before Augustus. Jerome also writes as follows about the Temple of Peace: *In the Temple of Peace that Vespasian and Titus built at Rome they dedicated vessels from the Jewish temple in its sanctuary together with all the gifts of the faithful, as the Greek and Roman historians relate.*[83] This single ignorant man wants his tract, written in barbarous language,

to be believed more than the most trustworthy histories of the most circumspect men of antiquity.

73   Since I have mentioned Jerome, I shall not allow the following insult to him to be passed over in silence: at Rome, on the authority of the Pope, a manuscript of the Bible is on display, like the remains of saints, with perpetual illumination because it is said that Jerome wrote it with his own hand. You ask for proof? It is true that there is considerable *painted cloth and gold*, as Virgil says[84] — something which would rather suggest that it was not written by the hand of Jerome. I myself, after careful inspection, discovered that it had been written by order of a king, Robert,[85] I think, in the handwriting of an inexperienced person. Similarly, although there are ten thousand instances of this kind at Rome, among the sacred objects are displayed the portraits of Peter and Paul on a panel which Sylvester put on show, when those apostles had appeared to Constantine in a dream, as a confirmation of the vision. I do not say this because I deny that those portraits of the apostles exist. I wish that Lentulus' letter about the image of Christ were as authentic,[86] even though it was no less knavishly forged than the grant that we have refuted. But I say what I say because that panel was not shown by Sylvester to Constantine.

74   In this matter I cannot contain my astonishment. Accordingly I shall say something about the legend of Sylvester, because the entire issue turns on this, and for me it will be fitting to speak above all about the Roman pontiff, since my discourse is concerned with Roman pontiffs, with a view to facilitating inferences about the others from this one example. Of the many absurdities that are told, I touch only upon the one about the dragon, in order to show that Constantine never had leprosy.[87] For the acts of Sylvester were written down by a certain Eusebius, a Greek man according to the testimony of the translator. That nation is always highly inclined to mendacity, as Juvenal says in a satirical assessment: *whatever the lying Greeks make bold to claim as history*.[88] Where

had that dragon come from? No dragons are born in Rome. Where too had his poison come from? Only in Africa are there supposed to be venomous dragons, because of the hot climate. Besides, where had so much poison come from so as to infect such a big city, particularly since the dragon was submerged in such a deep cave that a hundred and fifty steps were required to get down to it. With the possible exception of the basilisk, serpents inject their poison and kill not by breathing, but by biting. When Cato was fleeing from Caesar across the midst of the sands of Africa with a substantial body of men, he did not see anyone of his companions, marching or sleeping, stricken down by the breath of a serpent. Nor did the people there consider the air pestilential on that account, and, if we may believe the myths, the Chimaera, Hydra, and Cerberus were commonly observed and touched with impunity. Why had the Romans not slain it before? "They could not," you declare. Yet Regulus killed a much larger serpent in Africa on the banks of the Bagrada.[89] In fact this one in Rome was easy to kill, for example by blocking the mouth of the cave. Were they unwilling to do this? In my opinion they worshipped it as a god, the way the Babylonians did. Why then did Sylvester not kill it as Daniel is said to have done, by binding it with a cord of hemp and wiping out its progeny forever?[90]

The fabricator of the legend did not want the dragon to be 75 killed for fear that the derivation from the story of Daniel would seem obvious. Yet if Jerome, a most learned and reliable translator, Apollinaris, Origen, Eusebius, and others maintain that the story of Bel is a fiction, if even the Jews do not know it in the original of the Old Testament, in other words if the most learned of the Latin writers, most of the Greeks, and certain Hebrews condemn it as a fable, shall I not condemn this story, which is inspired by it, when it is supported by the authority of no writer and greatly surpasses its model in idiocy? Who had built the subterranean dwelling for the beast? Who had put the creature in it and instructed it

not to go out or fly away? (Dragons fly, they say, although some deny this.) Who had imagined that kind of food for it? Who had bidden women—virgins at that, and priestesses—to go down there, and only on the first of the month? Did the dragon know what day that was? Was he satisfied with such modest and infrequent feeding? Were not the virgins terrified of such a deep cave and of such an immense and ravenous beast? The dragon was nice to them, I suppose, as one would be to women, to virgins, and to people bringing food. I suppose he also chatted with them. What if—excuse my language—he even had sex with them? For both Alexander and Scipio are said to have been born from the intercourse of a dragon or serpent with their mothers. If food were denied him afterwards, why would he not have come forth and expired? How amazing the folly of men, who can put their faith in such old-wives tales!

76   How long had this been going on? When did it start? Before the advent of the Savior, or subsequently? No one knows. We should be ashamed, we should be ashamed of this silliness and frivolity beyond anything in theatrical shows. A Christian, who calls himself a child of truth and light, should blush to utter things that are not only not true, but not even plausible. "But," they say, "demons gained this power among the pagans to mock those who served the gods." Be quiet, you utterly ignorant people, not to say criminals, who invariably draw a veil like this over your stories. Christian candor has no need to shelter under falsehood. It is defended enough and more than enough on its own through its light and truth without those lying and flashy tales that are profoundly insulting to God, to Christ, and to the Holy Spirit. Had God so turned over the human race to the will of demons that they would be seduced by such obvious, such imperious miracles, to such an extent that he could almost be accused of injustice for having entrusted sheep to wolves, and men would have a signal excuse for their errors? But if the demons had so much licence before, they

would have even more now among the infidels. We see that this is not at all the case, and no stories of this kind are advanced by them. I shall say nothing of other peoples: I shall speak about the Romans, among whom very few miracles are reported, and these both ancient and uncertain.

Valerius Maximus says that the chasm in the ground in the 77 middle of the forum closed up again when Curtius, urging on his horse, had precipitated himself into it in full armor, and that it immediately returned to its pristine shape.[91] Likewise when the statue of Juno Moneta was jokingly asked by a certain Roman soldier after the capture of Veii whether she would like to move to Rome, she replied that she would.[92] Livy, an earlier and more serious author, knows neither of these stories.[93] He maintains that the chasm was there all along and was not a sudden opening but an ancient one, even before the foundation of the city, and was called Lake Curtius, because Curtius Mettius, a Sabine fleeing an onslaught of Romans, had hidden in it. And he maintains that Juno nodded, but did not speak in reply, and that the utterance she gave was a later addition to the story.[94] As for the nod, it is plain that they lied, either because they interpreted a motion of the statue — they were pulling it away — as made of its own accord, or they invented her nodding with the same jocularity with which they interrogated the hostile and conquered stone goddess. In fact Livy does not say that she nodded, but that the soldiers shouted that she had. Good writers do not defend these as facts but excuse them as reports, just as Livy himself says: *This allowance is granted to antiquity, that by commingling the human with the divine it may make the origins of cities more grandiose,*[95] and elsewhere: *But in such ancient history I would be satisfied if whatever is like the truth be accepted as truth. All this is more suited to theatrical spectacle, which loves miraculous events, than to reliability, and it is not worthwhile either to affirm or refute it.*[96] Terentius Varro, an author who is earlier in time, more learned, and, in my opinion, more serious, says that three versions of the

history of Lake Curtius have been handed down by as many authors—one by Proculus, that the lake was named for Curtius
himself, who threw himself into it; a second by Piso, that it was
named for Mettius the Sabine; and a third by Cornelius, with
whom he associated Luctatius, that it was named for Curtius the
consul, whose colleague was M. Genutius.⁹⁷ Furthermore, I would
not conceal that Valerius Maximus cannot quite be reproved for
speaking as he does, since a little later he adds solemnly and seriously: *With reference to the motion and utterance of immortal gods as perceived by human eyes and ears, I am not unaware how uncertain is the
opinion on which judgment is based. But since nothing new is said here and
only tradition is reported, authors should make their own claim to credibility.* As to the *utterance of the gods,* he spoke about Juno Moneta and
the statue of Fortune, which is twice imagined as speaking in these
words: *Duly have you seen me, matrons, duly have you dedicated me.*⁹⁸

78   But our own story-tellers indiscriminately bring in talking statues, about which pagans themselves and idolators say nothing.
They repudiate such stories more strenuously than the Christians
affirm them. Among pagans the very small number of miracles
does not depend upon the trustworthiness of authors but, as it
were, upon a certain holy and venerable claim of antiquity. Among
Christians relatively recent miracles are recounted, even though
those who lived at that time knew nothing about them. I do not
impugn admiration of the saints nor deny their divine works, since
I know that as much faith as a mustard seed can move even moun-
tains.⁹⁹ On the contrary, I defend and protect those works, but I
refuse to let them be confused with made-up stories. I cannot be
persuaded that those writers were anything other than infidels,
who did this in mockery of the Christians—to see if these fictions
would be conveyed by treacherous men into the hands of the ignorant and accepted as true—, or believers aspiring to imitate God
but without knowledge, men who were bold enough not only to
write about acts of the saints but to compose irresponsible pseud-

epigrapha on the Mother of God and Christ himself. The supreme pontiff calls these books Apocrypha, as if there were nothing wrong with an unknown author, — as if the stories told were
believable, — as if they were sacred and served to strengthen religion, so that now whoever approves something bad is no less cul-
pable than the person who made it up. We detect spurious coins,
we separate them out and throw them away: shall we not detect
spurious teaching, but rather hold on to it? Shall we mix it up
with good teaching and defend it as good?

For my part, to speak candidly, I deny that the Acts of Sylvester   79
are apocryphal, because, as I have said, a certain Eusebius is al-
leged as author, but I consider them false and not worth reading,
not only in other points but particularly in what is related about
the dragon, the bull, and the leprosy, which I have done so much
to refute. If Naaman was a leper, we shall not say straightaway
that Constantine was too. Many authors have mentioned the former case, but about the latter, involving the ruler of the world, no
one, not even one of his own citizens, has written, unless some
foreigner did. Eusebius should be trusted no more than someone
writing about the wasps that nested in Vespasian's nostrils and the
frog to which Nero gave birth (hence the report that the Lateran
acquired its name because the frog was lurking in the tomb).[100]
Neither wasps themselves nor frogs, if they could talk, would have
said this. I pass over the report that boys' blood cures leprosy,
which medicine does not acknowledge,[101] unless this is a reference
to the Capitoline gods, as if they had a habit of talking and had
ordered this treatment.

But why should I be surprised that the pontiffs did not under-   80
stand these things, when they are ignorant about their own name?
They claim that Peter was called Cephas because he was the
"head" of the apostles, as if this word were Greek from *kephalē*,
and not Hebrew or rather Syriac. The Greeks write *Kēphās, which
among them is translated* as *Petros*,[102] not "head." "Petrus / Petra" is

a Greek word, and *Petra* is stupidly explained by a Latin etymology as meaning "trodden underfoot." The pontiffs distinguish a metropolitan from an archbishop and want the former to be derived from the size of the city, although in Greek it is not "metropolis" but *mētropolis*, that is — mother state or city. They explain patriarch as if "father of fathers," Pope by the interjection *pape*, orthodoxy as if meaning "of right glory," and *Simonem* with shortening of the middle vowel, when it ought to be pronounced long, as in *Platonem* and *Catonem*, and many other similar errors that I omit, lest I seem to be charging all the supreme pontiffs with the mistakes of some.

81   Let these points be made, so that no one may wonder why many popes were unable to grasp that the Donation of Constantine was a forgery, even though in my opinion this deception originated with one of them.

: V :

82   "But," you say, "why do the emperors not deny the Donation of Constantine, since it worked to their detriment, instead of acknowledging, affirming, and preserving it?" Substantial point — marvelous defense! But which emperor are you talking about? If you mean the Greek, who was the true emperor, I shall deny the admission, but if you mean the Latin, I shall gladly admit it. For who is unaware that the Latin emperor was gratuitously installed by a supreme pontiff, Stephen (I believe)?[103] He stripped the power of the Greek emperor because he would not come to the aid of Italy, and he named a Latin one, with the result that the emperor received more from the Pope than the Pope from the emperor. To be sure, Achilles and Patroclus divided up the treasures of Troy according to certain arrangements among themselves

alone. The words of Louis seem to me to point to this sort of thing, when he says:

> I, Louis, Roman emperor, Augustus, by our confirmatory agreement do decree and grant to you, blessed Peter, prince of apostles, and through you to your vicar, Lord Pascal, the supreme pontiff, and to his successors in perpetuity, just as you have had under your power and sway from our predecessors until now, the following: the state of Rome with its duchy and suburbs as well as its villages, the mountain territories as well as sea coasts and ports, and all cities, castles, walled towns, and villas in the area of Tuscany.[104]

Louis, are you really making an agreement with Pascal? If all this belongs to you, in other words the Roman empire, why are you granting it to someone else? If it belongs to Pascal and is his possession, what is the point of the confirmation? How much Roman empire will you have left, if you lose the capital itself? The Roman emperor is so called from the name of Rome. Tell me, is everything else you possess yours or Pascal's? Yours, I suppose you will say: therefore the Donation of Constantine is invalid if you are the owner of what he gave the pontiff. If it is valid, by what right does Pascal turn all the rest over to you after retaining for himself only what he already possesses? What is the sense of such largesse involving the Roman empire, either yours to him or his to you? You therefore rightly speak of an agreement as if it were a kind of collusion. "But what I am going to do?" you say, "Shall I recover by armed force what the Pope is holding? But he has now become more powerful than I am. Shall I recover it by legal action? But my legal right is no more than he wants it to be. I did not come to the empire by inheritance, but by an agreement that if I wanted to be emperor I should make various promises to the Pope in return. Shall I say that Constantine gave away nothing of his empire? In that way I would be making a case for the Greek emperor and

would be cheating myself of all imperial rank. The Pope's rationale in making me emperor is that I am, as it were, his vicar, and if I fail to make promises he will not do this, and if I fail to obey he will depose me. As long as he gives to me, I shall admit to anything, I will agree to anything. Only believe me — if I actually owned Rome and Tuscany, I would not be acting as I am now. Pascal would be chanting in vain the tune of the Donation, since I consider it a forgery. It is not my business to look into the legal rights of the Pope, but it is the business of the emperor in Constantinople."

83   You are altogether forgiven in my eyes, Louis, and every other ruler in your position. What must we suspect about the agreements that other emperors have made with supreme pontiffs, when we know what Sigismund did, an otherwise excellent and very courageous man, and yet less courageous under the impact of his age? We saw him in Italy encompassed by just a few retainers and living from day to day, about to die of starvation in Rome if Eugenius had not given him food — but at the price of extorting the Donation. When he had come to Rome to be crowned emperor of the Romans, he could not have been crowned by the Pope without acknowledging the validity of the Donation of Constantine and making a donation of everything all over again.[105] What is more contradictory than for someone to be crowned a Roman emperor when he had renounced Rome itself? And to be crowned by a man whom he acknowledges and, to the extent it lies with him, makes the lord of the Roman empire? And to consider valid a donation which becomes true only if the emperor has nothing left of his empire? In my view, not even children would have done such a thing. So it is hardly surprising if the Pope takes upon himself the coronation of a Caesar, which ought to be the responsibility of the Roman people.

84   If you, Pope, can deprive the Greek emperor of Italy and the western provinces and create the Latin emperor, why do you make

use of agreements? Why do you divide up Caesar's property? Why do you transfer the empire to yourself? Therefore anyone who is called emperor of the Romans should know that in my judgment he is neither Augustus nor Caesar nor emperor if he lacks full power at Rome, and that if he makes no effort to recover the city of Rome he is clearly guilty of perjury. Those former Caesars — Constantine first among them — were not forced to take the oath by which today's Caesars are bound. As far as human resources allowed, they would take away nothing from the size of the Roman empire and would zealously augment it. But this is not why they were called Augusti, because they were supposed to augment the empire (as some think in their ignorance of Latin), for Augustus is called, so to speak, "sacred" from the gustatory habits of those avians that were customarily used in taking the auspices. The Greek language attests this as well, since among Greeks Augustus is called *Sebastos*, from which Sebastia takes its name.[106] Better for the supreme pontiff to be called Augustus, from augmenting, except that in augmenting his temporal resources he reduces his spiritual ones. So you see that the worse the supreme pontiff, the more he insists on defending this donation. Such was Boniface the Eighth, who tricked Celestine by pipes inserted into the wall.[107] He writes about the Donation of Constantine and despoiled the king of France, whose very kingdom he decreed to have been and to be subject to the Roman church, just as if he wanted to implement the Donation of Constantine. His successors, Benedict and Clement, immediately revoked this as wicked and unjust.

But, Roman pontiffs, what is the meaning of that anxiety of 85 yours in demanding that the Donation of Constantine be confirmed by one emperor after another, unless you mistrust your own legal authority? But, as the saying goes, you are washing a brick. For that donation never existed, and what does not exist cannot be confirmed. Whatever the Caesars give, they do because

they are deceived by the example of Constantine. They are unable to give the empire.

86   All right, let us suppose that Constantine gave and Sylvester was at one time in possession, but that later either he himself or one of his successors was removed from possession. (I am talking now about what the Pope does not possess, and I shall talk subsequently about what he does possess.) What more can I grant you than to concede that what never existed and could not have existed, did exist? Even so, I say that neither divine nor human law enables you to effect a recovery. In ancient law a Hebrew was forbidden to be a slave to a Hebrew for more than six years, and also every fifty years everything returned to its original owner:[108] in the time of grace shall a Christian be oppressed in eternal slavery by the vicar of Christ, who redeemed us from slavery? What should I say: will he be recalled to slavery after he has been made free and long enjoyed his freedom? I keep quiet about how savage, how violent, how barbarous the domination of priests often is. If this was unknown previously, it has recently been recognized from that depraved monster, Giovanni Vitelleschi, cardinal and patriarch, who wearied the sword, by which Peter had cut off the ear from Malchus, with the blood of Christians.[109] This is the sword by which he too died. Did the people of Israel truly have permission to revolt from the house of David and Solomon, whom prophets sent by God had anointed, because their burdens were overwhelming? Did God approve what they did, while we in the face of such tyranny will not have permission to revolt, especially from those who are not kings and cannot be, and from those who were shepherds of sheep—that is, of souls—and have become thieves and robbers?

87   To turn to human law, who is unaware that there is no legal right conferred by war, or, if there is, it has force only so long as you are in possession of what you gained by war? For when you lose possession, you have lost your legal claim. That is why no one customarily goes to court to recover captive prisoners if they have

escaped. The same is true of booty, if the former owners have recovered it. Bees and certain other kinds of flying creatures cannot be recovered if they have flown away a considerable distance from my private property and settled in someone else's. When it comes to human beings — not only free creatures but masters over others — will you try to reclaim through legal action those who have asserted their freedom by force and weapons, just as a person would do to reclaim his cattle, and not by force and weapons? Nor can you say to me: "The Romans justly waged war upon nations, and they justly deprived them of liberty." Do not bring me into that debate, lest I be compelled to speak against my fellow Romans. Yet no offense could have been so serious as to warrant peoples' everlasting slavery, since they have often waged wars through the fault of a prince or some great citizen in the state and then, after being defeated, were undeservedly penalized with slavery. The world is full of examples of this sort of thing.

Nor in truth is it assured by the law of nature that one people   88
subjugate another. We can instruct others and exhort them. We cannot rule over them and do them violence, unless, abandoning our humanity, we want to imitate the wilder beasts which impose their bloody rule upon the weaker, as the lion upon quadrupeds, the eagle upon birds, and the dolphin upon fish. But even these creatures do not make claims upon their own kind, but upon lesser breeds. We ought to do this all the more, and a man should scrupulously respect another man, since as Quintilian said, *no creature on earth is so fierce that it does not revere the likes of itself.*[110] There are therefore four reasons for making war: 1) to avenge a wrong and defend friends, 2) fear of incurring a disaster in the future if the strength of others is allowed to grow, 3) the expectation of booty, 4) a desire for glory. Of these the first is, to some extent, honorable, the second less so, and the last two in no way at all. In fact wars were frequently launched against the Romans, but after they had defended themselves they waged wars against their ene-

mies and others too, and no nation has come under their domination without being conquered and subjected in war—how rightly or for what reason is theirs to know. I would not wish to condemn them for having fought unjustly, nor to acquit them for acting justly. I would only say that that the Romans made war on others for the same reason as most peoples and kings, and that those who were attacked and conquered in war had the same license to defect from the Romans as they had from other masters, so that all authority not be assigned—something no one would accept—to the most ancient peoples, who were the first masters, in other words, to those who first took away the property of others. And yet the Roman people had a stronger claim over nations conquered in war than the emperors who demolished the Republic. Accordingly, if was right for nations to revolt from Constantine and, even more, from the Roman people, it will certainly be right to revolt from the man to whom Constantine surrendered his authority. To speak more boldly, if the Romans were free to expel Constantine as they did Tarquin or to kill him as they did Julius Caesar, all the more will the Romans and the provinces be free to kill that man, whoever he may be, who has taken Constantine's place.

89   True as this is, it goes beyond my subject, and therefore I want to restrain myself and not exploit anything that I have said except this: it is foolish to apply a verbal claim where there is armed force, because anything acquired by force is lost by force. All the more since other new nations (as we have learned about the Goths), nations never subject to Roman rule, have occupied Italy and many provinces after driving out the original inhabitants: what is the justice in making them slaves, which they never were, particularly since they are victors and would perhaps be slaves of the people they conquered? At that time, if any cities and nations which were deserted by the emperor, as we know happened, considered it necessary, as the barbarians were approaching, to choose a king under whose leadership they won a victory, should they depose this man

from his position? Should they order his sons, esteemed as much for their father's advocacy as for their own virtue, to be reduced to private status? So that they might be once again subject to a Roman emperor, particularly when they were in great need of the sons' support and hoped for help from no other source? If that emperor or Constantine were to come back to life or the Senate and the Roman People were to summon them to a general tribunal, such as the Amphictyons had in Greece, he would be immediately rebuffed on his first plea, because he was calling back into dependence and slavery those who had been formerly deserted by him as their protector, those who had been living for a long time under another ruler, those who had never been subject to a foreign king, those who were, in short, born to freedom and laid claim to their freedom by the strength of their minds and bodies. Hence it is clear that if the emperor and the Roman people are excluded from reclaiming their control, the Pope is excluded much more decisively, and if other nations that were under Rome are free either to create their king or maintain a republic, the Roman people is much more free, especially in opposition to a new kind of tyranny, the Pope's.

: VI :

Our adversaries, who have been kept from defending a donation that never was and, even if it had been, would have collapsed over the course of time, resort to another form of defense, and, as if they had retreated from their city, gather themselves into the citadel, which they are compelled to surrender just as soon as the food runs out. "The Roman church," they say, "has exercised its authority in those territories it possesses." Why, therefore, does it lay claim to those territories—which constitute the greater part—over which it has not exercised any authority, whereas others have?

Unless the freedom the church enjoys towards others is not granted to others towards itself.

91   *The Roman church has exercised its authority*: Why, therefore, is it so often concerned that this right be confirmed by the emperors? Why does it boast of the donation and the imperial confirmation, if just one of these would suffice? You do wrong by not keeping quiet about the second justification. So why do you not keep quiet about it? Obviously because the Donation is insufficient on its own.

92   *The Roman church has exercised its authority*: How can it have done this, when it is based on no title but only on possession in bad faith? If you deny possession in bad faith, you certainly cannot deny in stupid faith. Or, in a matter so great and so conspicuous, ought ignorance of fact and law to be excused? Fact—because Constantine did not give Rome and the provinces: an ordinary person might be unaware of this but not the supreme pontiff. Law—because those places could not have been given or accepted: one could scarcely be a Christian and not know this. Will stupid credulity give you a right to what would never have been yours, had you been more prudent? Now at least, after I have demonstrated that you had possession through ignorance and stupidity, will you not forfeit that right, if you ever had it? Will not knowledge provide a salutary removal of what your ignorance unfortunately brought to you, and will not your estate go back from an unjust master to the just, perhaps even with interest? But if you persist in keeping possession, your ignorance is straightaway transformed into malice and deceit, and you plainly become a possessor in bad faith.

93   *The Roman church has exercised its authority*: You untutored innocents in divine law! No amount of years, no matter how many, can wipe out a legitimate title. If I had been captured by barbarians and thought to have died, would I have been shut out, after a hundred years in captivity, when I returned home again to claim my

paternal inheritance? What would be more inhumane than this? And, to introduce another example, did Jephtha, the leader of Israel, answer the Ammonites who claimed the land *from the borders of the Arnon to the Jabbok and the Jordan*,[111] "Israel has already exercised its authority there for three hundred years"? Or did he show that the land they claimed had never belonged to them but to the Amorites, and that the proof it did not belong to the Ammonites lay in their never having asked for it back over the course of so many years?

The Roman church has exercised its authority: Be still, wicked 94 tongue! You transfer to man an authority that is exercised over mute and mindless objects. The longer a man is kept in slavery, the more detestable it is. Birds and wild animals do not want to be subject to authority, but however long they have been confined, as soon as the occasion presents itself, they escape as they like. Will a man, when possessed by a man, not be free to escape? Hear why the Roman pontiffs who make use of war, not law, to achieve their justice display fraud and treachery more than ignorance. In my opinion the first pontiffs behaved similarly in occupying the city of Rome and other towns. Shortly before I was born — I call upon the memory of those who were there — by an unexampled kind of deceit Rome accepted the rule of the Pope, or rather his tyranny, when for a long time the city had been free. The Pope was Boniface the Ninth, equal to the Eighth in fraud as well as in name (if in fact the worst malefactors have to be called Bonifaces), and when the Romans became outraged after the treachery was uncovered the good Pope, like Tarquin, shook off all the highest poppy flowers with his stick. Subsequently, when Innocent, the man who succeeded him, wanted to imitate this act, he was driven from the city.[112] I have no desire to talk about the other pontiffs who held Rome in continuous subjection by force of arms, although it rebelled as often as it could, just as it did six years ago: When the city could not obtain peace from Eugenius and, being

under siege, was no match for its enemies, it laid siege to the Pope himself inside his house and would not allow him to go out before he either made peace with the enemy or turned over the administration of the state to citizens. But he preferred to abandon the city by assuming a disguise and taking along one companion in flight, rather than to accede to the citizens in their just and equitable demands.[113] If you give them a choice, who does not know that they would choose freedom over slavery? One may suspect that it would be no different for other cities that are held in slavery by the supreme pontiff, by whom they ought rather to have been liberated from slavery. It would take a long time to enumerate how many cities, captured from the enemy, the Roman people formerly made free, to such an extent that Titus Flaminius ordered the whole of Greece, which had been subject to Antiochus, to be free and enjoy its own laws.[114] But the Pope, as may be observed, assiduously plots against the liberty of peoples. Therefore, as the occasion arises, they rebel in turn every day—look at Bologna recently.[115] If any of them ever voluntarily consented to papal rule—which can happen when some danger is threatening from another quarter, it must not be imagined that they consented to make themselves slaves, that they could never pull their necks out from under the yoke, that afterwards they and their offspring would have no jurisdiction over themselves. This would be foully unjust. Voluntarily, supreme pontiff, we came to you to govern us: voluntarily we now go away from you, lest you govern us any longer. If we owe you anything, a balance sheet of credits and debits can be drawn up. But you want to govern us against our will, as if we were your charges, whereas we would perhaps be able to govern you more wisely than you can.

95   Add to this the wrongs that are inflicted upon this city all the time by you and your magistrates. God knows, wrongdoing compels us to revolt, as Israel did from Rehoboam in the past. Yet what was so great a wrong for it—paying heavier taxes—is only a

part of our disaster. What if you bankrupt our republic? You have done it already! If you rob our temples? You have done that too! If you violate virgins and mothers? That too you have done! If you spatter the city with civil blood? You have already done that! Must we endure this? Or rather, if you stop being a father to us, shall we forget that we are also your sons? The people summoned you, supreme pontiff, as a father or — if you like this better — as a master, but not as an enemy and executioner. You have no desire to play the role of father or master, but of enemy and executioner. We will not imitate your cruelty and your impiety, even though under the law of reprisal we could, since we are, after all, Christians, nor will we draw our avenging swords against your person, but after your abdication and removal we will adopt another father or master. Sons are free to escape from wicked parents who gave them birth. Will we not be free to escape from you — not a true father but an adoptive one who is treating us outrageously? As for you, look after your sacral duties. Do not enthrone yourself in the North and thunder from there as you hurl bolts of lightning against this people and all others.

But why should I say anything more in a case that is utterly 96 transparent? I not only assert that Constantine did not give away so many territories and that the Roman pontiff could not have had any authority in them, but also, if either proposition were true, it would be cancelled by the crimes of the possessors, since we see that the ruin and devastation of all Italy and many provinces have flowed from this one source. If the source is bitter, so is the stream. If the root is contaminated, so are the branches. If the first fruit is not pure, neither is the whole product. So, in reverse, if a stream is bitter, the source must be blocked. If branches are contaminated, the problem comes from the root. If a whole product is impure, the first fruit must be shunned as well. Can we justify the principle of papal power, when we observe it to be the cause of so

many crimes and of so many evils of every kind? Accordingly I say and shout out—for I shall have no fear of men since I trust in God—that in my time no one in the office of supreme pontiff has been either *a faithful or a prudent steward*.[116] He is so far from giving food to God's own people that *he has eaten them up like food*[117] and a crust of bread. The Pope himself makes war on peaceful nations and sows discord among states and rulers. The Pope thirsts for the goods of others, in the way that Achilles described Agamemnon, *dēmoboros basileus*,[118] "a people-devouring king." The Pope not only makes a profit from the republic, which not even Verres, Catiline, or any other embezzler dared to do, but also from the church and the Holy Spirit, which even the notorious Simon Magus refused to do. When he is advised of all this and censured by certain good men, he makes no denial but openly acknowledges it and boasts of it. He claims he is allowed to separate by any means the patrimony bestowed by Constantine upon the church from those who have possession of it, as if the Christian religion would be blessed by his taking it over and not more oppressed by every kind of crime, indulgence, and licentiousness, provided that it could still be more oppressed and more criminality could still be accommodated. In order to take over all the other parts of the donation, he spends the money he has foully stolen from good citizens for even more foul purposes by underwriting the cavalry and infantry forces that infest everything, as Christ lies dying of starvation and exposure among so many thousands of poor. He fails to realize— a most unworthy misdeed—that, when he strives to take away from secular officers what is theirs, they in turn are either induced by his deplorable example or compelled by necessity, although perhaps not genuine necessity, to take away what belongs to ecclesiastical officers. And so there is no longer any scruple, no sanctity, no fear of God, and, *I tremble to say this*,[119] wicked men find an excuse for all their crimes in the Pope. For he and his companions furnish an example of every kind of misdeed, so that with Isaiah and Paul

we can declare to the Pope and those close to him: *Through you the name of God is blasphemed among the nations. You who teach others do not teach yourselves. You who preach against theft are robbers. You who abominate idols commit sacrilege. You who glory in the law* and in the pontificate *dishonor God,* the true pontiff, *by transgressing the law.*[120] But if the Roman people lost, in consequence of excessive wealth, its true Romanness, if Solomon slipped for the same reason into idolatry through consorting with women, do we not recognize that the same thing is happening to the supreme pontiff and the rest of the clergy? Do we then imagine that God would permit Sylvester to accept the wherewithal for committing sin? I will not suffer this injury to be done to a most holy man, I will not tolerate this insult to be addressed to an excellent pontiff, so that he may be said to have accepted empires, kingdoms, and provinces, which those who want to become clergy normally renounce. Sylvester had few possessions, as did all the other holy pontiffs, whose appearance struck awe even among their enemies, just as the sight of Leo terrified and broke the savage spirit of a barbarian king when Roman forces had been unable to do this.[121] But recent supreme pontiffs, who are awash in riches and luxuries, seem to work hard to be as wicked and foolish as their predecessors were wise and holy, and to overwhelm the outstanding reputations of former pontiffs with every kind of disgrace. Who that considers himself a Christian can bear this with equanimity?

But in this first speech of mine I do not wish to encourage rul- 97
ers and peoples to restrain the Pope as he surges ahead in his unbridled course and to force him to stay within his own borders, but only to counsel him, when perhaps he has already recognized the truth, to move back voluntarily from a house that is not his own into the one where he belongs and into a haven from irrational tides and cruel storms. But if he should refuse, then we shall gird ourselves for a second, much more aggressive speech. I wish, how I wish that one day I might see — indeed, I can scarcely wait

to see, particularly if it is carried out on my initiative — that the Pope is the vicar of Christ alone and not of the emperor as well, and that those dreadful phrases are heard no more: the church faction, the anti-church faction, the church fighting against Perugia, against Bologna. The church does not fight against Christians. It is the Pope who does. The church fights against *spiritual wickedness in high places.*[122] At that time to come the Pope will be called, and really will be, Holy Father, father of all, father of the church. He will not provoke wars among Christians but, through apostolic censure and papal majesty, bring an end to the wars provoked by others.

APPENDIX
THE DONATION OF
CONSTANTINE[1]

In the name of the Holy and Indivisible Trinity — Father, Son, 1
and Holy Spirit, in Jesus Christ, our one Savior, Lord, and God
from that Holy Trinity, Flavius Caesar Constantine, the faithful,
gentle, greatest, benevolent, Alamannic, Gothic, Sarmatic, Ger-
manic, Britannic, Hunnic, pious, fortunate, victor and triumpha-
tor, ever august, to the very holy and very blessed father of fathers,
Sylvester, bishop of the city of Rome and pope, and to all his successors who will be sitting upon the seat of the blessed Peter down
to the end of time, to the pontiffs and all very reverend and catholic bishops beloved of God, who are subject to the same sacrosanct
Roman church through this our imperial constitution, those in
office now and in all time still to come: grace, peace, charity, joy,
forbearance, pity from God, the omnipotent Father, and His Son
Jesus Christ, and the Holy Spirit be with you all.

What our Savior and Redeemer, Lord God Jesus Christ, Son 2
of the loftiest Father, has judged worthy of miraculous accom-
plishment through his holy apostles Peter and Paul, with the intervention of our father Sylvester, supreme pontiff and universal
pope, our very gentle Serenity has studied to disseminate throughout the whole world in a pellucid account by this our imperial decree for the enlightenment of all peoples. Firstly our faith, which
we have learned from the aforementioned very blessed father and
our orator, Sylvester, the universal pontiff, we are advancing for
the instruction of the minds of all of you through an intimate confession of the heart, and thereby declaring the pity of God that
has been spread over us.

3   We want you to know, just as we have signified by our earlier holy pragmatic order, that we have withdrawn from the worship of idols, deaf and dumb images made by hand, devilish devisings and all the pomp of Satan, and have attained the spotless faith of Christians, which is the true light and life everlasting, believing, according to the instruction we received from the greatest nourishing father and our teacher the pontiff Sylvester, in God the Father omnipotent, and in Jesus Christ, his only Son, our Lord God through whom all things have been created, and in the Holy Spirit, the Lord and generator of all creation. We acknowledge these, the Father and the Son and the Holy Spirit, such that the plenitude of divinity and the unity of power may be in a perfect Trinity: God the Father, God the Son, and God the Holy Spirit, and the three are one in Jesus Christ. Thus three forms, but one power.

4   For the wise God has forever produced from himself the Word by which the ages had always to be brought forth, and when by only that same Word of wisdom He formed all creatures out of nothing, He was with it, arranging everything according to His own secret mystery. Therefore when He had made the glories of the heavens and all the materials of the earth, at the pious bidding of His wisdom He first created man from the mud of the ground in His image and likeness and placed him in a paradise of pleasure. The old serpent and envious enemy, the devil, rendered him an exile from those very delights through the exceedingly bitter taste of the forbidden tree, and once man was expelled the serpent did not cease from casting his poisonous darts in manifold ways, so that by deflecting the human race from the path of truth he might persuade it to submit to the worship of idols, that is — of what was created rather than the Creator, whereby through those whom he was able to enmesh in his plots he brought it about that they would be burned with him in everlasting torment. But our God, compassionate for the creature he had formed, dispatched

His own holy prophets, through whom He announced the light of life to come—the advent of His own Son, our Lord God and Savior Jesus Christ, and He sent His only begotten Son and the Word of wisdom. Descending from the heavens for the reason of our salvation, born of the Holy Spirit and the Virgin Mary, He became the Word made flesh and dwelt among us. He did not lose what He had been, but began to be what He was not, perfect God and perfect man, as God working miracles and as man enduring human sufferings. Thus, as our father Sylvester, the supreme pontiff, preached the true man and the true God, we understand that we are in no way doubtful that He was true man and true God. Having chosen twelve apostles, He shone by his miracles before them and a multitude of innumerable people. We acknowledge that the same Lord Jesus Christ fulfilled the law and the prophets, that having suffered and been crucified He was resurrected from the dead on the third day according to the Scriptures, that having been taken up into the heavens and sitting on the right hand of the Father, thence will come to judge the living and the dead, and of His reign there will be no end.

For this is our orthodox faith as transmitted to us by our most 5 blessed father, Sylvester, the supreme pontiff. On this account are we exhorting all people and the various nations of races to embrace this faith, to practice and preach it, and to take up the grace of baptism in the name of the Holy Trinity, and to adore with a dedicated heart Lord Jesus Christ our Savior, who lives and reigns for infinite ages with the Father and the Holy Spirit, whom our most blessed father Sylvester, the universal pontiff, preaches.

Our Lord God Himself, pitying me, a sinner, sent His holy 6 apostles to visit us, and the light of His splendor gleamed over us, and you congratulate me, having been taken out of the darkness, that I have reached the true light and recognition of the truth. For when a strongly foul leprosy had invaded all the flesh of my body and many doctors who were brought in took care of me, I did not

recover my health at the hands of any one of them. Priests of the Capitol came to address the matter, declaring that I had to have a tub built on the Capitol and have it filled with the blood of innocent infants, and that I could be cleansed in this warm bath. A large number of innocent infants were rounded up according to their words, while the sacrilegious priests were arranging for them to be slaughtered and the tub to be filled from their blood, Our Serenity saw their mothers' tears. I was immediately horrified by the deed and, pitying them, we ordered their sons to be restored to their parents. With the provision of carriages and the granting of gifts, in joy we sent them home.

7   Once the day was over, in the silence of night when the hour for sleeping had come, the apostles, holy Peter and Paul, are with me, saying: "Since you put an end to crimes and were horrified by the spilling of innocent blood, we have been sent by Christ, our Lord God, to give you advice for recovering your health. Hear, therefore, our counsels and do whatever we tell you. Sylvester, bishop of the city of Rome, fleeing your persecutions as far as Mount Serapta, is cultivating a hiding place with his clergy in stone caves. When you have brought him to you, he will show you a pool of piety in which, as he immerses you for the third time, all that strength of the leprosy will leave you. When this has happened, reward your Savior for this change, so that all the churches in the whole world may be revived on your order. As for yourself, purify yourself in this manner — that, once you have abandoned all superstitious worship of idols, you adore the living and true God, who is the only God and true, and see to it that you follow His will."

8   Rising from sleep, I immediately accomplished what I had been counselled by the holy apostles to do. When that distinguished and fostering father and our illuminator, Sylvester, the universal pope, had been summoned, I revealed all the instructions I had received from the holy apostles, and we asked him who those gods

were: Peter and Paul? He replied that they ought not to be called gods but apostles of our Savior, the Lord God Jesus Christ. And again we began to ask the same most blessed pope whether he possessed a depiction of those apostles, so that we might learn from the picture that these were the ones that the revelation had presented to me. Then the venerable father ordered that the images of those same apostles be displayed by his deacon. When I saw these images and had recognized in them the countenances of those whom I had seen outlined in my sleep, with a huge cry in front of all my satraps I acknowledged that they were the ones whom I had seen in my sleep.

Whereupon that most blessed Sylvester, our father, bishop of the city of Rome, imposed on us a penitential time within our Lateran palace in one room in a hair shirt, so that for everything that had been impiously transacted by us and unjustly administered we would, by vigils, fastings, and tears, and by prayers through our Lord God Jesus Christ, our Savior, obtain forgiveness. Then, by way of imposition of the hands of the clergy, I came to the prelate himself, and there renouncing the pomp of Satan and his works, as well as all idols made by hand, I professed, of my own free will before all people, that I believe in God the Father omnipotent, Maker of heaven and earth, of things visible and invisible, and in Jesus Christ, his only Son, our Lord, who was born of the Holy Spirit and of the Virgin Mary. And after blessing the font he purified me in the salubrious water by a threefold immersion. There, as I was placed in the embrace of the font, I saw with my own eyes as a hand came down to touch me from heaven. I rose up clean. You see that I am now cleansed of all the foulness of leprosy. When I was taken up from the venerable font and clothed in white garments, he granted the unction of the blessed *chrisma* with the sign of the sevenfold Holy Spirit upon me, and he drew on my forehead the sign of the Holy Cross, saying: "God marks you with the seal of his faith in the name of the Father and

9

the Son and the Holy Spirit, as a token of faith." The entire clergy responded: "Amen." The prelate added: "Peace be with you."

10   And so on the first day after I received the mystery of the sacred baptism and the healing of my body from the foulness of leprosy, I recognized that there is no other god than the Father and the Son and the Holy Spirit, Whom the most blessed Sylvester preaches, Trinity in unity and unity in Trinity. For all the pagan gods, which I have worshipped hitherto, are shown to be demons, hand-wrought works of men, and the venerable father expounded to us most lucidly how great a power our Savior conferred upon his blessed apostle Peter in heaven and on earth, when finding him faithful in interrogating him He says, "You are Peter, and upon this rock I will build my church, and the gates of Hell will not prevail against it."[2] Take note, you powerful ones, and listen with the ear of your heart to what the Good Teacher and Master added when he said to his disciple: "And I will give you the keys of the kingdom of the heavens; and whatever you bind together on earth will be bound also in the heavens, and whatever you loosen on earth will be loosened in the heavens."[3] This is wondrous indeed and glorious — to bind and to loosen on earth, and to be bound and loosened in heaven.

11   While I was recognizing these things through the preaching of the blessed Sylvester and I ascertained that I had been wholly restored to health through benefits accorded by the blessed Peter himself, we have judged it useful, together with all our satraps and the entire Senate, and the Optimates too, along with all the Roman people subject to the glory of our empire, that, just as he is seen to have been established as the vicar of the Son of God on earth, so too should the pontiffs who hold the place of the Prince of the Apostles obtain from us and our empire the concession of a princely power of greater extent than the clemency of our earthly imperial Serenity appeared to possess,[4] choosing the very Prince of the Apostles, or his vicars, to be strong advocates for us with God.

And as our imperial power is earthly, we have decreed honor with veneration for his sacrosanct Roman church and that the most sacred seat of the blessed Peter be gloriously exalted more than our empire and earthly throne, in that we assign to him power, the dignity of glory, and the vigor and distinction of empire.[5]

And we sanction by decree that he have primacy over the four 12 distinguished sees of Antioch, Alexandria, Constantinople, and Jerusalem as well as over all churches of God in the whole globe of earth. Furthermore, the pontiff who in the course of time has stood over the sacrosanct Roman church shall exist as loftier and leader to all the priests of the entire world, and whatever pertains to the worship of God or to guaranteeing the stability of the faith of Christians shall be arranged according to his judgment.[6] It is indeed just that where the institutor of holy laws, our Savior, ordered the blessed Peter to have his apostolic seat, there holy law should maintain the capital of the principate—that where shouldering the cross he drank the cup of blessed death and appeared as an imitator of his Teacher and Lord, there peoples should bend their neck in confessing the name of Christ, where their teacher the blessed apostle Paul was crowned with martyrdom after extending his neck for Christ; there they should seek their teacher unto the end, where the sacred body of the teacher rests, and there, prostrated and bowed down, they should carry out their duty towards the heavenly king, our Savior God, Jesus Christ, there where they used to be subject to the rule of a proud earthly king.

In the meantime we want all peoples of all races and nations 13 throughout the whole world to know that we have built inside our Lateran palace a church with its own foundation and baptistery for our Savior, Lord God, Jesus Christ, and you should know that from its foundation we have carried on our own shoulders twelve bags filled with earth in accordance with the number of the twelve apostles. We prescribe that the sacrosanct church be designated, honored, venerated, and proclaimed as the head and summit of all

churches in the entire world, just as we have legislated through our other imperial decrees. We have built churches of the blessed Peter and Paul, the first apostles, which we have enriched with gold and silver, where burying their most sacred bodies with great honor we have also constructed their coffins out of amber, against which no force of the elements prevails. And we have put a cross of purest gold and precious gems on their individual coffins and fastened them shut with golden keys. For these we have granted properties of our possessions to guarantee the lights, and we have enriched those churches with various items, and by our sacred imperial ordinances we have granted them a largesse no less in the east than in the west and even in the northern and southern sectors, that is — in Judaea, Greece, Asia, Thrace, Africa, and Italy as well as various islands, on this express condition that everything be in the hands of our most blessed father Sylvester, the supreme pontiff, and his successors.[7]

14 Let all people rejoice with us, and nations of races in the whole world. We exhort everyone to give immense thanks with us to our God and Savior, Jesus Christ, since God Himself, in the heavens above and in the earth beneath, visiting us through His holy apostles, made us worthy to received the holy sacrament of baptism and bodily health. For this we grant to those holy apostles, our lords, the blessed Peter and Paul and through them to the blessed Sylvester, our father, the supreme pontiff and universal pope of the city of Rome, and to all his successor pontiffs, who will be sitting in the seat of the blessed Peter until the end of the world, and as of now we hand over the Lateran palace of our empire, which ranks above and surpasses all other palaces, in the entire world, then the diadem — that is, the crown on our head and at the same time the Phrygian tiara and the superhumeral band (which is the strap that normally goes around the imperial neck), but also the purple cloak and the scarlet tunic and all imperial vestments, or the rank of commanders of the imperial cavalry. We confer on him

as well the imperial sceptres and at the same time pikes and standards and banners and various imperial decorations, and every procession of our imperial eminence and the glory of our power.[8]

And for very reverend men, clergy of different ranks serving the 15 holy Roman church, we sanction that pinnacle, exceptionality, authority, and prominence with whose glory our most illustrious Senate seems to be adorned, namely to be made patricians and consuls, and we promulgate that they be decorated in all other imperial dignities. Just as the imperial militia exists as decorated, so have we decreed that the clergy of the holy Roman church be adorned. Just as the imperial authority is decorated by different offices — chamberlains indeed, door-keepers, and all bed-mates, so do we wish the holy Roman church to be decorated.[9] In order that the pontifical splendor may gleam most brilliantly, we also decree that the clergy of the same holy Roman church — that their horses be decorated and ridden with napkins of linens that are of the whitest color, and that they be distinguished in the same way as our Senate, which makes use of shoes with felt socks — that is, with white linen. Thus will the celestial ranks be adorned like the terrestrial, to the glory of God.[10] Before all else, however, we assign to our very holy father, Sylvester, bishop of the city of Rome and Pope, and to all most blessed pontiffs who come after him in succession and in perpetuity, for the honor and glory of Christ our God in the same great catholic and apostolic church of God, the right to name to the clergy anyone he wishes from our Senate at his pleasure and by his own decision and to include that person in the pious ranks of the pious clergy, and that no one whatsoever should consider that he is acting arrogantly.[11]

And so we have also decreed the following: that our father, the 16 venerable Sylvester, supreme pontiff, and all his successors ought to use the diadem — that is, the crown — made of purest gold and of precious gems, which we have granted to him from our own head, and to wear it on their head to the glory of God and for the

honor of blessed Peter.[12] But the most holy Pope himself did not suffer the use of that crown of gold on top of the priestly crown,[13] which he wears to the glory of the most blessed Peter. But we have placed with our own hands upon his most holy head a Phrygian tiara of white radiance, as a symbol of our Lord's splendid resurrection, and holding his horse's bridle out of reverence for the blessed Peter we have assumed for him the role of a squire, as we ordain that all his successor pontiffs individually use the same tiara in processions in imitation of our imperial power.[14]

17   Accordingly, to ensure that the pontifical preeminence not be demeaned but adorned with a glorious power greater than the dignity of imperial rule, behold — we give over and we leave to the most blessed pontiff and universal Pope, our father Sylvester, and to the power and sway of him and his successor pontiffs, not only our palace, as has been revealed, but the city of Rome and all the provinces, places, and cities of Italy or the western territories, and by a firm imperial decision through this our sacred divine rescript and pragmatic sanction we have decreed that they be managed and we grant that they should remain under the law of the holy Roman Church.[15]

18   Wherefore we have considered it appropriate for our empire and kingly power to be transferred and transmuted for the eastern territories, and in the best place of the province Byzantia for a state to be built named for us and our empire to be established there.[16] For where the prince of priests and the head of the Christian religion has been established by the heavenly ruler, it is not just for the earthly ruler to have power there.

19   Furthermore, everything that we have established and confirmed through this sacred imperial charter and through other divine decrees we decree to remain untouched and unaltered down to the end of the world.[17] Accordingly before the living God, who ordered us to reign, and before his terrible judgment seat we entreat[18] through this our imperial constitution all our successors,

emperors and every nobleman, satraps too and the most resplendent Senate and the entire people in the entire world that is subject to our rule now and in all time to come, to permit none of them in any way either to oppose or demolish these things that have been granted by us through imperial sanction to the sacrosanct Roman church and all its pontiffs or for these to be torn asunder in any way.[19] If, moreover, anyone — which we do not believe — emerges as a falsifier or scorner in this context, let him be bound up and subjected to eternal damnation. Let him know that his enemies are the holy first apostles of God, Peter and Paul, in the present and in the life to come, and let him be burned in the lower reaches of hell and waste away together with the devil and all who are wicked.[20]

Reinforcing the page of this our imperial decree by our very own hands, we have placed it on the venerable body of the blessed Peter, first of the apostles. There pledging to that apostle of God to conserve all these things inviolate and to leave them under orders to our successor emperors to be conserved, we have handed them over to the most blessed Sylvester, our father, supreme pontiff, and universal Pope, and through him to all his successor pontiffs, with the assent of the Lord God and our Savior Jesus Christ, to be possessed forever and prosperously.

The imperial subscription:

May the Divinity preserve you for many years, most holy and blessed fathers.

Given at Rome on the third day before the Kalends of April, when the distinguished consuls were our lord Flavius Constantine Augustus for the fourth time and Gallicanus.[21]

Note on the Translations

꙾꙾꙾

The translation of Valla's *On the Donation of Constantine* in this volume is based on the Latin text of Wolfram Setz in volume 10 of the *Quellen zur Geistesgeschichte des Mittelalters* in the *Monumenta Germaniae Historica* (Weimar, 1976). The translation of *The Donation of Constantine (Constitutum Constantini)* is based on the text established by H. Fuhrmann, *Das Constitutum Constantini (Konstantinische Schenkung)* in the *Monumenta Germaniae Historica, Fontes*, vol. 10 (Hannover, 1968).

Notes

☙❧

ABBREVIATIONS

MGH   Monumenta Germaniae Historica

PL   *Patrologiae cursus completus, series Latina,* ed. Jacques-Paul
Migne, ed., 221 vols. (Paris: Migne, 1844–1891).

ON THE DONATION OF CONSTANTINE

1. Cf. Macrobius, *Saturnalia* 2. 3. 21, recording that Asinius Pollio, who had written verses against Augustus during the triumviral period, decided to hold his tongue for the reason Valla gives. The precise quotation is "It is not easy to write . . ."

2. Psalms 139:7.

3. Echoing Matthew 18:15.

4. I Timothy 5:20.

5. Galatians 2:11.

6. For 'becoming one spirit with God' see I Corinthians 6:17. Valla's source for the story about Pope Marcellinus I (not Marcellus) is probably the *Liber pontificalis* 30; the less plausible accusation that Celestinus I agreed with the heretic Nestorius may be an inference from the correspondence between Celestinus and Nestorius (*PL* 50. 438–444). The "certain persons" "rebuked by persons of inferior status" were the popes deposed and/or condemned by the Councils of Constance and Basel.

7. John 10:11, with Psalms 58:4–5.

8. Already in late antiquity Constantine was believed to have planned first to build his new city in the vicinity of Troy in Asia Minor: Zosimus 2. 30 (cf. Sozomen 2. 3. 2), presumably at the site of Alexandria Troas, where Julius Caesar had planned a colony, Antony established one, and Augustus reinforced it: M. Ricl, *The Inscriptions of Alexandria Troas* (Bonn,

1997), pp. 21–21 and 224–225. The story lived on in the *Historia Tripartita* 2. 18. 2.

9. Virgil, *Aeneid* 1. 151. Valla has reversed Virgil's word order (*pietate gravem*).

10. Livy 5. 24, 8–10.

11. Livy 1. 58.

12. The citations from Paul come from I Corinthians 9:15 and Romans 11:13, respectively. The two previous quotations are from Acts 20:35 and Matthew 10:8.

13. The Biblical quotations in this paragraph are from I Timothy 6:7–11, Matthew 6:19 and Matthew 19:24.

14. II Timothy 2:4. For the refusal of the apostles to serve at table see Acts 6:2.

15. Jeremiah 48:10.

16. John 21:15–17.

17. John 18:36.

18. Matthew 4:17 and Mark 1:15.

19. Cf. Mark 4:30.

20. Matthew 20:25–28.

21. The speaker is assuming the traditional identification of the nation of Israel with the Christian church, the "new Israel."

22. I Corinthians 6:2–4.

23. Matthew 17:26.

24. Matthew 21:13 and John 12:47. Both the Greek Testament and the Vulgate give *save* in place of *free*.

25. Matthew 26:52.

26. Matthew 26:51.

27. Matthew 16:18–19 (Valla has reversed the order of the verses).

28. Matthew 4:9.

29. Ephesians 6:17.

30. Matthew 11:29–30.

31. Matthew 22:21.

32. *Digest* 50. 17. 69: *invito beneficium non datur*, ascribed to the jurist Paul.

33. Eutropius, *Breviarium* 10. 9. 1. Perhaps for stylistic reasons, Eutropius identifies the Iranian rulers as Parthians, which they were not. They were the Parthians' successors, the Sassanian Persians.

34. Eutropius, *Breviarium* 10. 17. 1–2. Sapor (Shapur II, 310–379) was the Persian Shah. Julian's successor, Jovian, made peace with him after Julian died in 363 on campaign against the Persians. Despite Valla's references to the Caudine Forks (321 BC), Numantia (153 BC), and Numidia (109 BC), he is wrong about the relinquishment of part of the Roman empire. Hadrian famously gave up territory conquered by his predecessor Trajan in a war against Parthia.

35. The antipope Felix V (Duke Amadeus VIII of Savoy), elected by the Council of Basel on 5 November 1439.

36. Valla has misread and misdated gold coins in his private collection so as to mean "concord of the world." In fact, the legend is CONOB or COMOB, and the coin first appears only in 369 under Valentinian I, several decades after Constantine's death. The OB in these legends abbreviates *obryza*, a word of obscure etymology to indicate pure gold. CON was initially a mint mark for Constantinople, combined with OB, but in coins of the western empire COM appeared, perhaps indicating *com(es)*, "count" in charge of gold. See J. Melville Jones, *A Dictionary of Ancient Roman Coins* (London, 1990), p. 65. Most specimens with a cross above the legend are known as *tremisses*. Since the B can be read as an R, Valla's reading presupposes CON(cordia) OR(bis).

37. *Decretum Magistri Gratiani* (ed. Friedberg), C XII q. 1, c. 15. The reference to Eusebius is to the *Ecclesiastical History* 9.9.1–12. Valla does not know, or chooses not to mention, Eusebius' *Life of Constantine* 1.27–32, where Constantine's conversion during his campaign against Maxentius in 312 is described.

38. The Donation of Constantine appears in Part I, Distinction 96, canons 13–14 of the *Decretum*, which was a part of the text added after the

time of Gratian (probably around 1150) by another hand. These additions, which included over 150 canons, were mostly made by law professors at the University of Bologna and were known as *paleae* ("chaff" or "straw"), though some writers later spoke as though the additions were made by a single compiler named Palea. Distinction 96 is attributed to a compiler nicknamed Paucapalea in canonist writers. Valla probably drew his information about the early text of Gratian from Nicholas of Cusa's *De concordantia catholica* 3.2 (see introduction). On the addition of the forgery to the *Decretum* see Weigand, "Fälschungen als Paleae"; on the evolution of Gratian's text, see A. Winroth, *The Making of Gratian's Decretum* (Cambridge, 2000).

39. R. Fubini, "Humanism and Truth," 82, claims that the "some [*nonnulli*]" is "an actual citation of Cusanus." Not likely, unless, as Fubini asserts, Valla misread Cusanus. And that is not at all likely.

40. *Decretum*, Dist. XCVI, c. 13.

41. Ibid., Dist. XV c. 3, 19.

42. Jacopo da Voragine (Vorazze), archbishop of Genoa, wrote a work called *The Golden Legend*. He died in 1298. Curiously, in the late fifteenth century, undoubtedly as a result of Valla's critique, someone inserted a reference to the Donation in the *Legend*: cf. Miglio, "L'umanista Pietro Edo," pp. 221–222, 229–232, cited by Black, "The Donation of Constantine," pp. 72–73.

43. See I Esdras 3–4 for the story of Darius and I Maccabees 8:20–22 for Judas Maccabaeus.

44. Josephus, *Jewish Antiquities* 1. 64.

45. *Decretum*, Dist. XCVI, c. 14.

46. Virgil, *Aeneid* 2. 77–79. Scholars today prefer the reading *fuerit quodcumque*.

47. This is one of the most damning anachronisms in the entire Donation. The word *satrap* was not applied to high officials in Rome before the mid-eighth century. See Wolfgang Gericke, "Wann entstand die Konstantinische Schenkung?" *Zeitschrift der Savigny-Stiftung*

für Rechtsgeschichte, Kanonistiche Abteilung 43 (1957), 1–88, especially p. 8, and now Wolfram Brandes, "The Satraps of Constantine," in Johannes Fried, *"Donation of Constantine" and "Constitutum Constantini"* (Berlin, forthcoming, 2007).

48. Tertullian, *Apologeticum* 5. 1–2, cf. 21. 24. Similarly, Eusebius, *Ecclesiastical History* 2. 2–5.

49. Cicero, *Pro Sestio* 96.

50. Sallust, *Catiline* 54.

51. Virgil, *Aeneid* 6. 851.

52. Gregory I, in MGH *Epistolae* 2: 263.

53. Christian author, teacher of Constantine's son Crispus, and a master of Latinity, known in the Renaissance as the Christian Cicero. He wrote *Divine Institutes* and *On the Death of Persecutors*. Valla admired him.

54. Apocalypse 5:12.

55. The word *princeps* (here "leader") was also the term used as equivalent to "emperor" in ancient sources and was applied to any sovereign ruler in the Renaissance.

56. Quoted by Quintilian, *Institutio oratoria* 4. 2. 91.

57. Psalms 86:15.

58. Psalms 81:12.

59. Romans 1:28.

60. Matthew 23:2.

61. Cf. Numbers 16:1.

62. Valerius Maximus, *Memorabilia* 7. 2. 5.

63. Plautus, *Menaechmi* 426; Pliny the Elder, *Natural History* 8. 196.

64. Matthew 27:28; John 19:2.

65. A snail rather than a fish. It belongs to the family of *muricidae*.

66. Homer, *Iliad* 17. 360–361; Virgil, *Aeneid* 9. 349.

67. Virgil, *Aeneid* 10. 640.

68. Phrase from Lucan, *Pharsalia* 1. 7.

69. Horace, *Ars Poetica* 97.

70. Julius Valerius, *Res Gestae Alexandri* I. 37.

71. Adapted from Virgil, *Georgics* 4. 121–122: *tortusque per herbam / cresceret in ventrem cucumis.*

72. Martial, *Epigrams* 14. 141. The allusion is to felt made of goat-hair from the region of Lepcis Magna and the adjacent Bay of Kinyps in North Africa. The manuscripts of Martial give the title of this two-line epigram as *Udones Cilicii* (Cilician socks), and the editor of the new Loeb edition of Martial ponders why the hair of North African goats should be referred to Cilicia. Valla's text provides the correct reading for the title in Martial: *Udones Cilicini*, i.e. hairy socks.

73. Psalms 20:4.

74. The title *papa* was used in the early Western church of any bishop and was applied even to priests in the Eastern church. The term *papacy* (*papatus*) is first used by Clement II in 1047, and the popes began to use the tiara and imperial robes only after 1059 (see Colin Morris, *The Papal Monarchy: The Roman Church from 1050 to 1250* [Oxford, 1989], 107, 130).

75. Xenophon, *Cyropaedeia* 1. 1. 321.

76. Homer, *Iliad* 2. 493–877. Valla had translated both the *Cyropaedeia* and the first sixteen books of the *Iliad*.

77. Matthew 5:18.

78. Apocalypse 22:18–19.

79. The Greek word for actor is *hupokritēs*. Valla plays on the prefix *hupo* (under).

80. Cf. Livy 3.31. 8. Francesco Accursio wrote glosses on the *Corpus iuris civilis*.

81. II Kings 15:5.

82. See Innocent III, *Sermones de sanctis*, PL 217.457.

83. Jerome (Hieronymus), *Commentaries on Joel* 3. 4–6 (PL 23. 270).

84. Virgil, *Aeneid* 9. 26.

85. Setz in his edition proposes Robert Guiscard, but Valla is more likely to have in mind Robert of Anjou, King of Naples (1277–1343), the patron of Giotto, Petrarch and Boccaccio.

86. A medieval forgery, perhaps from the thirteenth or fourteenth century. See Cora E. Lutz, "The Letter of Lentulus Describing Christ," *Yale University Library Gazette*, 50 (1975), 91–97.

87. Cf. W. Pohlkamp, "Tradition und Topographie: Papst Silvester I. (314–335) und der Drache vom Forum Romanum," *Römische Quartalschrift* 78 (1983), 1–100.

88. Juvenal, *Satires* 10. 174–175.

89. Pliny, *Natural History* 8. 36; Valerius Maximus, *Memorabilia* 1. 8. 19.

90. The story of Bel and the Dragon is contained in one of the apocryphal or deutero-canonical books of the Bible.

91. Valerius Maximus, *Memorabilia* 5. 6. 2.

92. Ibid., 1. 8. 3.

93. Livy, 1. 12. 10; 13. 5. Cf. 7. 6.

94. Livy, 5. 22. 5.

95. Livy, Preface 7.

96. Livy, 5. 21. 9.

97. Varro, *De lingua latina* 5. 148–150.

98. Valerius Maximus, *Memorabilia* 1. 8. 7 and 1. 8. 4.

99. Cf. Matthew 17:19.

100. *Golden Legend* 65 and 79. The fictitious etymology exploits the Latin words *rana*, "frog," and *latere*, "to lie hidden."

101. But the elder Pliny (*Nat. Hist.* 26. 8) reports that in Egypt elephantiasis patients were put in bathtubs warmed with human blood.

102. John 1: 42. Cephas is Peter's name in Aramaic, and *Petros*, rock, is the Greek equivalent.

103. The imperial title was "transferred" to Charlemagne by Pope Leo III on Christmas Day, AD 800.

104. Valla quotes an imperial charter of Louis the Pious of 817, but from what source is unclear. The text is edited in the *Capitularia regum francorum*, ed. A. Boretius, MGH Legum Sectio II (Hannover, 1883), 1: 353, no. 172.

105. The coronation of Sigismund of Luxembourg as Holy Roman Emperor took place in Rome on 31 May 1433.

106. Presumably a reference to the city of Samaria in Palestine, later known as Sebastia.

107. Valla refers to a story that Boniface had a pipe inserted into the wall of the prison in which Celestine was confined. An apparently celestial voice spoke through it to urge the Pope to abdicate. See F. Gregorovius, *Geschichte des Stadt Rom im Mittelalter* (Dresden, 1926), 2: 520.

108. Deuteronomy 15:12 and Leviticus 25:10.

109. Vitelleschi was archbishop of Florence, patriarch of Alexandria, cardinal of San Lorenzo in Damaso, and legate of Eugenius IV in Rome. Notorious for his monstrous character, he was overthrown and arrested in March of 1440. He died of wounds on 2 April 1440. Since Valla completed the present work by 25 May of that year (cf. his letter to Giovanni Tortelli, cited in the Introduction), the downfall of Vitelleschi must have occurred as he was writing or shortly before.

110. The quotation, which Valla ascribes to Quintilian himself (M. Fabius Quintilianus), occurs in Pseudo-Quintilian, *Declamations* 12. 27. It appears again in Valla's *Elegantiae* 2. 53.

111. Judges 11:13.

112. Both Boniface IX (pope 1389–1404) and Innocent VII (pope 1404–06) tried to limit the independence of the Commune of Rome and both were expelled from the city at various times by popular uprisings. For Tarquin and the poppies, see Livy 1. 54. 6.

113. In 1434 a popular uprising in Rome forced Eugenius to flee Rome by boat, disguised as a monk. But the ruse was found out and Eugenius was pelted by stones from both banks of the Tiber before escaping to Ostia and Florence. Eugenius was still in Florence at the time Valla's oration

was written (hence the words about Eugenius being "enthroned in the North").

114. Valla has the name wrong. Flaminius should be Flamininus. But the history is correct: see Livy 33. 32 and Plutarch's *Life of Flamininus* ch. 10. The date was 196 BC.

115. In 1428 the papal legate was expelled from Bologna.

116. Luke 12: 42.

117. Psalms 53: 4.

118. Homer, *Iliad* 1. 231.

119. Virgil, *Aeneid* 2. 204.

120. Isaiah 52: 5; Romans 2: 21–23.

121. Leo I's appearance before Attila the Hun in 452 is said to have led to Attila's withdrawal from Italy.

122. Ephesians 6: 12.

APPENDIX: THE DONATION OF CONSTANTINE

1. Valla did not subject the first ten sections of this document to the withering analysis he devoted to the terms of the actual gift. But the Latinity of those sections is no less vulnerable, abounding in infelicities, mistakes, pleonasms, and anacolutha. For example, in §5 observe the absurd redundancy of *in omnem populum et diversas gentium nationes*, or the absolute nominative participle *exhortantes* that serves as main verb. Valla could have been eloquent on *nocturna nobis facta silentia* with which §7 opens. But I do not believe that even this forger could have written *pontificalis decus* in §15, as printed by Fuhrmann, especially with strong manuscript support for *pontificale decus*. In the new fascicle of the *Mittellateinisches Wörterbuch*, III.1 (Munich, 2000) s.v. *decus*, only three examples of masculine *decus* are mentioned among the vast number of examples in cols. 134–137, and of those three two are but variant readings (including the *Constitutum* example).

2. Matthew 16:18.

3. Matthew 16:19.

4. Valla's text of this section is slightly different, notably with *cuncto populo Romano gloriae imperii nostri subiacenti* replaced by *cum cuncto populo imperio Romane ecclesie subiacenti*. Valla also gives simply *vicem* after *apostolorum* without the relative *qui* and *gerunt vices*.

5. Valla's quotation of these lines is likewise slightly different, notably showing *gloriam et dignitatem* for *gloriae dignitatem* in Fuhrmann's text.

6. Valla's text of these lines omits the adjective *praecipuas* before the patriarchal seats, and, more interestingly, lists the seats in a different order: Alexandria, Antioch, Jerusalem, Constantinople. His text also reads *ad cultum Dei et fidem christianorum vel stabilitatem procurandam* in place of Fuhrmann's *ad cultum dei vel fidei Christianorum stabilitate procuranda*. Valla mocks *vel* as it appears in his text.

7. In this sentence Valla reads *continuatione* in place of *concinnatione*, and *per nostram imperialem iussionem sacram* in place of *per nostras imperialium iussionum sacras*. His text is preferable in both places. For the redaction of the Gratian text used by Valla, see Johanna Petersmann, "Die kanonistische Überlieferung des Constitutum Constantini bis zum Dekret Gratians," *Deutsches Archiv für Erforschung des Mittelalters* 30 (1974), 356–449, especially on Gratian 389ff., a reference that I owe to the kindness of Professor Fuhrmann.

8. Valla reads *cuncta* for *et conta atque*, and *banda* for *banna* — better readings on both counts, again probably corrections made by copyists.

9. Valla's text of this section is noticeably different: it begins with *Viris etiam diversi ordinis*, and and for the succession of accusatives *culmen* through *praecellentiam* he reads *culmen* with dependent genitives *singularis potentie et precellentie*. *Promulgantes* becomes *promulgavimus* in Valla. *Decernimus* in Fuhrmann becomes *decrevimus* in Valla. The word *concubitorum*, which Valla mocks, is *excubiorum* in the *Constitutum* (not that this would change Valla's point), and Valla's *ordinatur* is *ornatu decoratur* here. Valla has *ita clerum sancte Romane ecclesie adornari decrevimus* for *ita et sanctam Romanam ecclesiam decorari volumus*.

10. Apart from minor verbal variants, Valla reads *mappulis et linteaminibus*, rather than *mappulis ex linteaminibus* as here, and for the grotesque

decoratos equos equitent, mocked by Valla, the *Constitutum* has the ungrammatical *decorari equos et ita equitari*. Similarly Valla reads *utitur* and *illustrentur* for *uti* and *illustrari* in Fuhrmann. Once again Valla's text shows corrections made in the manuscript transmission.

11. The final part of §15 is drastically abbreviated, and much improved, in Valla's text. The prolix naming of Sylvester together with his successors and the church itself is cut back to just a few words. Valla includes, however, the phrase *ex nostro indictu* after the reference to Sylvester's successors. Fuhrmann's apparatus leads one to suppose that this is a correction of *ex nostra synclitu* in the *Constitutum*, since *synclitu* is sometimes replaced with *inclitu*, *inclitis*, or *inclyto*. In Fuhrmann's Leo-Humbert group of manuscripts all display *ex nostro indictu*. In general, Valla's text seems to have the closest affinity to that group.

12. Again Valla's text of these lines is salubriously abridged, but the *videlicet* phrase and the reference to gold and gems, which both provoked Valla's indignation, survive.

13. The tonsure. This sentence appears almost intact in Valla (apart from his *beatus* for *sanctissimus*).

14. Valla reads *splendidum* for *splendidam*, *imposuimus* for *posuimus*, *dextratoris* for *stratoris*. He omits *pontifices* before *singulariter*. At the end of the sentence the word order is inconsequentially changed in Valla's text to *ad imperii nostri imitationem*.

15. The barbarous Latin of the text as constituted at this point by Fuhrmann had been considerably cleaned up by the time of the manuscript that was available to Valla. In particular, *gloriae potentia* in the *Constitutum* has been replaced with *gloria et potentia*, *Romae urbis* with *Romanam urbem*, *contradentes atque relinquentes* with *tradimus atque relinquimus*, and above all by the replacement of everything from *eius vel successorum* through *sacram et* with *ab eo et a successoribus eius per*.

16. Valla's text is close to the *Constitutum* here, although *transmutari* has disappeared.

17. Valla's text shows inconsequential tense variants in this sentence, e.g. *decrevimus* for *decernimus*.

18. Valla omits *per hoc nostrum imperialem constitutum* at this point.

19. The second half of this sentence is substantially abridged in Valla's text. Most of the phrase from *nunc* to *subiacenti* has gone apart from *in posterum*, *haec* has become *hoc*, and the long phrase *quae . . . concessa sunt* is completely missing. So is *refragare*.

20. There are two interesting variants in Valla: *contemptor* is missing, and *innodatus* is replaced with *condemnatus*.

21. The subscription as given by Valla is more precise in that it specifies both Constantine and Gallicanus as consuls for the fourth time. It also omits the honorific *viris clarissimis* as well as Constantine's *nomen gentile*. But this subscription is far more damning than even Valla could have imagined. The emperor Constantine was never consul in the same year with Gallicanus. Gallicanus served in 330 with Aurelius Valerius Tullianus Symmachus. Constantine had been consul in the previous year, but for the eighth time, not the fourth. In that year his colleague was none other than his own son, also called Constantine, who was actually consul then for the fourth time. See T. D. Barnes, *The New Empire of Diocletian and Constantine* (Cambridge, Mass., 1982), p. 96. The forger mixed up two different years and two Constantines. See also the final note to the introduction in the present volume.

Bibliography

ﷺ

TEXTS

The Treatise of Lorenzo Valla on the Donation of Constantine. Translated by Christopher B. Coleman. New Haven, 1922. Reprinted Toronto, 1993. With a Latin text.

Lorenzo Valla. *De falso credita et ementita donatione declamatio.* Edited by Walter Schwahn. Leipzig, 1928. Reprinted Stuttgart, 1994.

Lorenzo Valla. *La falsa donazione di Costantino (contro il potere temporale dei Papi).* Translated by Gabriele Pepe. Milan, 1952. Italian translation with notes.

Das Constitutum Constantini (Konstantinische Schenkung). Edited by Horst Fuhrmann. MGH Fontes, vol. 10. Hannover, 1968.

Lorenzo Valla. *De falso credita et ementita Constantini donatione.* Edited by Wolfram Setz. MGH, Quellen zu Geistesgeschichte des Mittelalters, vol. 10. Weimar, 1976.

Laurentii Valle Epistole. Ed. Ottavio Besomi and Mariangela Regoliosi. Padua, 1984.

Lorenzo Valla. *The Profession of the Religious and the Principal Arguments from the Falsely-Believed and Forged Donation of Constantine.* Translated and edited by Olga Zorzi Pugliese. Toronto, 1985. Partial English translation only.

Lorenzo Valla. *La donation de Constantin (sur la Donation de Constantin, à lui faussement attribuée et mensonger).* Translated with a commentary by Jean-Baptiste Giard. Preface by Carlo Ginzburg. Paris, 1993.

SECONDARY LITERATURE

Antonazzi, Giovanni. *Lorenzo Valla e la polemica sulla Donazione di Costantino, con testi inediti dei secoli XV-XVII.* Rome, 1985.

Black, Robert. "The Donation of Constantine: A New Source for the Concept of the Renaissance." In *Languages and Images of Renaissance Italy,* ed. A. Brown, pp. 72–73. Oxford, 1995.

Gericke, Wolfgang. "Wann entstand die Konstantinische Schenkung?" *Zeitschrift der Savigny-Stiftung für Rechtsgeschichte*, Kanonistiche Abteilung 43 (1957): 1–88.

Bowersock, G. W. "Peter and Constantine." In *St. Peter's in the Vatican*, ed. W. Tronzo, pp. 5–15. Cambridge, 2005.

Camporeale, Salvatore I. "Lorenzo Valla e il *De falso credita donatione*: Retorica, libertà ed ecclesiologia nel '400." *Memorie domenicane* n.s. 19 (1988): 191–293.

Idem. "Lorenzo Valla's *Oratio* on the Pseudo-Donation of Constantine: Dissent and Innovation in Early Renaissance Humanism," *Journal of the History of Ideas* 57 (1996): 9–26.

Fried, Johannes. *"Donation of Constantine" and "Constitutum Constantini": The Misinterpretation of a Fiction and its Original Meaning*. With a contribution by Wolfram Brandes, "The Satraps of Constantine." Berlin, forthcoming, 2007.

Fubini, Riccardo. "Contestazioni quattrocentesche della Donazione di Costantino: Niccolò Cusano, Lorenzo Valla." In *Costantino il Grande dall' antichità all' umanesimo*, ed. G. Bonamente and F. Fusco, 1: 385–431. Macerata, 1992.

Idem. "Humanism and Truth: Valla Writes against the Donation of Constantine." *Journal of the History of Ideas* 57 (1996): 79–86.

Miglio, Massimo. "L'umanista Pietro Edo e la polemica sulla Donazione di Costantino." *Bulletino dell' Istituto storico italiano per il medioevo* 79 (1968): 167–232.

Setz, Wolfram. *Lorenzo Vallas Schrift gegen die Konstantinische Schenkung*. Bibliothek des Deutschen Historischen Instituts in Rom, 44. Tübingen, 1975.

Weigand, Rudolf. "Fälschungen als Paleae im *Dekret* Gratians." In *Fälschungen im Mittelalter*, MGH Schriften 33.2, pp. 301–318. Hannover, 1988.

Index

꿩§꿩

Numbers in roman type refer to paragraphs of Valla's work; numbers preceded by "A" refer to paragraphs of the Appendix. Italicized numbers (roman and arabic) refer to pages in the Introduction and Notes.

Publication of this volume has been made possible by

The Myron and Sheila Gilmore Publication Fund at I Tatti
The Robert Lehman Endowment Fund
The Jean-François Malle Scholarly Programs and Publications Fund
The Andrew W. Mellon Scholarly Publications Fund
The Craig and Barbara Smyth Fund
for Scholarly Programs and Publications
The Lila Wallace–Reader's Digest Endowment Fund
The Malcolm Wiener Fund for Scholarly Programs and Publications